HYDROPONICS
(SOILLESS CULTURE OF PLANTS)

Dr. Dharm Singh
M.Sc. Ag., Ph.D., FASA (USA), M.H.Sc. (London)
Managing Director
Indian Medicinal Plants Marketing Federation,
New Delhi

AGROBIOS (INDIA)

Published by:
AGROBIOS (INDIA)
Agro House, Behind Nasrani Cinema
Chopasani Road, Jodhpur 342 002
Phone: 91-0291-2642319, Fax: 2643993
E. mail: agrobios@sify.com

AGROBIOS (INDIA)

ISBN (10): 81-7754-329-6
ISBN (1[illegible]) 978[illegible]4-3292
Price: R[illegible]S. **30.00**

9 788177 543292
Rs. 1200.00 / US$ .00
Published by:
AGROBIOS (INDIA)

Published by: Dr. Updesh Purohit for Agrobios (India), Jodhpur
Laser typeset at: Yashee Computers and Printers, Jodhpur
Cover Design by: Reena
Printed at: Bharat Printing Press, Jodhpur

Tel / Fax : 23383549
E-mail : ag.comm@nic.in

कृषि आयुक्त
भारत सरकार
कृषि मंत्रालय
(कृषि एवं सहकारिता विभाग)
कृषि भवन, नई दिल्ली-110001
Agriculture Commissioner
Government of India
Ministry of Agriculture
(Department of Agriculture & Cooperation)
Krishi Bhawan, New Delhi-110001

FORWORD

Soil is the best growing medium for the plants. It provides nutrients, water and anchorage for successful growth of the plants. Sometimes, soil poses a serious limitation for desired growth of the plants, due to unsuitable soil reactions, unfavourable properties and presence of harmful insects and disease pathogens. Moreover, continuous cultivation of crops in a same piece of land and erosion hazards has a drastic reduction in soil fertility which after some times makes soil unfits for plants. On other hand, it is very difficult for plant hobbyists to grow ornamental and other kind of plants in metropolitan cities due to lack of sufficient space, scarcity of water and availability of costly labour inputs. In such situation, hydroponic offers an opportunity for gardeners to grow wide range of plant species very successfully with less labour, less water and low investments.

Hydroponics is a unique system of gardening in which large space, more labour, large volume of water and oil for nutrient supply/support are not required. This technique provides the best possible environment to the plants leading to their fast growth, quality produce, higher yields and early returns. Hydroponic plants are typically more healthy, mature earlier and there are no weeds to deal with.

This book deals with different key issues of hydroponics and its proven as well as adoptable technologies which can be great asset to its readers. Dr. Dharm Singh, Managing Director, Indian Medicinal Plants Marketing Federation, deserves great appreciation, which has made commendable efforts in writing this very useful book.

I congratulate Dr. Singh for bringing out this very useful contribution to all the people who have an access to soil and water conservations, clean environment healthy life and sufficient food.

(N.B. Singh)

PREFACE

Hydroponics refers to methods of growing plants in a water and nutrient solution, without soil. This technique allows gardeners to grow plants in a more efficient and productive manner with less labour and time required. In the Hydroponic system of plants growing, the nutrients are directly fed at the root base, never stressing the plant due to lack of nutrients or water. This technique is ideal for growing wide range of plant species especially fruit bearing crops, such as tomatoes, cucumbers, and peppers, leafy crops like lettuce, cabbage, herbs and flowering plants. Hydroponics offers an opportunity to provide optimal conditions for plant growth with higher yields as compared to open field agriculture. This technique can be used any where in all agro-climatic zones and hydroponic produce has higher nutritional value and tastes better than field growing crops. The cost of production in Hydroponics is also less over conventional methods. If optimum growing conditions and nutritional requirements are applied, combined with sound horticultural management, this system of growing plants can offer an alternative means of food production.

Due to various advantages over open field agriculture, Hydroponics is more popular in some countries like Canada, especially in commercial production of vegetables. But in India, this technique could not get popularity among gardeners till the date. The main bottleneck behind this is lack of its standard knowledge and poor dissemination of its available technologies. Although, more literature on Hydroponics is available but standard, precise and authentic information's are still lacking.

For popularization of Hydroponics in our country, it is very important to provide scientific proven technology of Hydroponics to gardeners and create mass awareness in potential areas at National level.

This book, based on my past year's experience of work done on hydroponics, is intended to provide practical and standard information's on various aspects in précised and digestible form. Various key issues have been discussed in different chapters to make it very useful to every gardener, farmer, student, scientist, planner and policy maker to gain enough knowledge of hydroponics required for successful and satisfactory growing plants.

In placing this book before you, I am immensely thankful to Dr. N.B Singh, Agriculture Commissioner, Government of India for providing the foreword.

I would like to express my heartfelt gratitude to Col. V.K. Sharma (Retd.), Chairman, Indian Medicinal Plants Marketing Federation, Dr. Punjab Singh, Vice-Chancellor, Banaras Hindu University, Varanasi (U.P.), Mrs., Manju Chauhan, Chairperson, National Honey Marketing Board, Dr. B.G. Shrivastava, Ex-Principal Scientist IARI, and Dr. Ram Chand, Assistant Director General (Agriculture Extension), ICAR for their inspiration, encouragement and sustained support. My special thanks are also due to Dr. S.S. Purohit and Dr. Updesh Purohit, Directors, Agrobios (India), Jodhpur (Rajasthan) and Mr. Vinod S Rawat, Computer Programmer of the federation for their all kind of support in preparation and publication of this manuscript.

Further, I would like to express my acknowledgements and thanks to all Authors whose papers, reports and books we have consulted in preparation of this text.

I am sure that this publication would not only be informative to the readers but also promote a concern, that every citizen of our country has an access to conserve water, a precious natural resource to mankind in recent years.

DR. DHARM SINGH

CONTENTS

1 **INTRODUCTION** **1**
Definition of Hydroponics 1
Why do People Prefer Hydroponics? 4

2 **HISTORY OF HYDROPONICS** **6**
Historical Highlights 14

3 **PRESENT STATUS AND FUTURE PROSPECTS OF HYDROPONICS** **16**
Present Status 16
Future Prospects of Hydroponics 18
Modern Hydroponics 21
Future Strategy of Hydroponics 22

4 **ADVANTAGE AND LIMITATIONS OF HYDROPONICS** **23**
Advantages of Hydroponics 23
Limitations of Hydroponics 25

5 **HYDROPONIC TECHNIQUES AND THEIR CLASSIFICATION** **27**
Classification 27
Hydroponic Techniques 28
1. Liquid Hydroponics 29

A. Circulatory Methods (Closed Systems) 29
a. Nutrient Film Technique - NFT *29*
b. Deep Flow Technique – DFT *31*
B. Non Circulating Methods (Open Systems) 34
a. Root Dipping Technique *34*
b. Floating Technique *36*
c. Capillary Action Technique *36*
2. Aggregate Systems 37
A. Hanging Bag Technique (Open System) 37
B. Grow Bag Technique 38
C. Trench or Trough Technique 40
D. Pot Technique 41
3. Aeroponics 41
A. Root Mist Technique (RMT) 42
B. Fog Feed Technique (FFT) 43
Other Techniques 43
1. The Ebb and Flow System 43
2. Drip System 44
3. Wick System 45
4. Deep Water Culture (DWC) 46
Drip Feeding 46
Wick Feeding 46
Raft Cultivation 46
Dynamic Root Floating System 46
Ridged Culture Bed 48
Concave Panel 48
Nutrient Level Adjuster and Aspirator 49
Nutrient Circulation System 50
Cropping Patterns 50
Cultural Practices 51
Nutrient Solution 52
Adjustment of Nutrients 53

6 BASIC REQUIREMENTS OF HYDROPONICS 55
1. Growing Media 56
2. Nutrient Solutions 56
3. Temperature 57

4. Fresh Air 57
5. Shelter and Support 57
6. Water 58
7. Mineral Nutrients 58
8. Light 59

7 GROWING MEDIA 61
1. Expanded Clay 61
2. Rockwool 62
3. Perlite 63
4. Vermiculite 64
5. Coco Coir 65
6. Oasis Root Cubes 65
7. Sand 66
8. Coarse Fir Sawdust 66
9. Crushed Granite 66
10. Scoria 67

8 EQUIPMENTS AND APPLIANCES 68
1. Water Pumps 68
2. Timer and Oxygen Detection Sensor 68
3. PVC Pipes 69
4. pH Meter 70
5. Blowers 70
6. Pollinators 71
7. Nurtimeter 71
8. EC Meter 71
9. TDS Meter 71

9 NUTRIENT SOLUTIONS FOR HYDROPONICS 73
Essential Plants Nutrients 73
Criteria used for Considering Elements as Essential 74
Individual Plant Nutrients of Hydroponic Solution 74
Nitrogen 74
Sulphur 74
Phosphorous 74
Potassium 75

Calcium 75
Magnesium 75
Iron 75
Boron 75
Zinc 76
Manganese 76
Copper 76
Molybdenum 76
Function of Minerals 76
1. Protoplasmic Elements 76
2. Balancing Elements 77
3. Framework Elements 77
4. Influence on the Osmotic Pressure of the Cells 77
5. Catalytic Elements 77
Nutrient Solution 77
Chelating Agents 78
Preparation of Nutrient Solution 79
Nutrient Solution Management 80
pH Level 81
Why is pH Important? 82
Checking of pH 84
Adjusting pH 85
Electrical Conductivity (EC) 86
Measuring Conductivity 86
Concentration of Dissolved Oxygen (DO) 87
Automatic Management of Nutrient Solution 88
pH 89
Measuring 89
pOH 90
Drip (Substrate) 92
Fertilizer Mixtures for Hydroponics 93
Hydroponic, Organic and Regular Fertilizers 94
Replacement of Nutrient Solution 95
Fertigation 95
Methods of Fertigation 96
Advantages of Fertigation 97
Factors to be Considered in Fertigation 97

Irrigation Water Quality 97
Standard Nutrient Solutions 99
D. R. Hoagland Standard Solution Method 99
Knop's Solution 101
Sach's Solution 101
Hogland Solution 101
Combination Developed by NBRI Lucknow for Vegetables and Floriculture 101
These Combination are Dissolved in 4.5 Liter of Water 102
Non Standard Solutions 102
Dissolve this Combination in one Liter of Water 102
How to Make Compost 104
Solution from the Soil 105

10 BIOPLANTOMIN – A SUCCESSFUL MEDIA FOR MODERN HYDROPONICS 107
What is Bioplantomin ? 108
What is Desert-Hydroponic ? 108

11 HYDROPONIC METHODS FOR NURSERY AND ORCHIDS GROWING 109
Nursery Raising 109
Requirements for Nursery Raising 109
1. Growing Media 109
2. Nursery Containers / Trays 111
3. Moisture 111
4. Relative Humidity 112
5. Ideal Temperatures 112
6. Light 113
Seed Germination 113
Planting Material Production 113
Nutrient Supply 114
Nursery Period 114
Sponge Nursery Technique 115
Semi-Hydroponic for Growing Orchids 116
Planting 116
Media 117

Water 117
Fertilizer 117
Conversion from Conventional Culture to Semi-Hydroponic 117
Transplantation 117
Suitable Orchids for Hydroponics 118
Advantages of Semi-Hydroponics 118
Disadvantages 118

12 SOURCE OF LIGHT 119

Light Spectrums 119
Artificial Lighting 120
Plant Light Needs 121
Lamp Placement 121
Types of Lights for Plant Growth 122
Incandescent Light 123
Fluorescent Light 123
Metal Halide Light 123
High Pressure Sodium Light 124
Visible Radiations Required for Photosynthesis 124
Working with Light 126
Photosynthetically Active Radiation (PAR) 128
Light Distribution 131
High-Intensity Discharge (HID) 132
Metal Halide 133
High-Pressure Sodium (HPS) 133
Electronic Ballasts 133
Different E-Ballasts such as Life Lights 133

13 TRAINING AND PRUNING 135

14 MANAGEMENT REQUIREMENTS OF HYDROPONICS 137

Care and Maintenance of Hydroponic Systems Recirculating Systems 139
Non-Recirculating Systems 139
Moisture Content 139

Flushing ... 140
High Temperature ... 140
Low Temperatures ... 140
Containers ... 140

15 PROBLEMS OF HYDROPONICS AND THEIR REMEDIES ... 141
Insect-Pest and Disease Problem ... 141
Physiological Disorders ... 142
Blossom End Rot of Tomato ... 142
Concentric Fruit Cracking of Tomato ... 143
Shrink Cracks of Bell Pepper ... 143
Fruit Crooking of Cucumber ... 144
Nutritional Disorders ... 144

APPENDIX
I Important Plant Diseases and their Symptoms ... 145
II Nutritional Deficiency Symptoms in Plants ... 147
III Nutritional Toxicity Symptoms in Plants ... 149
IV Suitable Plants for Hydroponics ... 151
V Essential Plant Nutrients ... 153
VI Constituents of Nutrient Solution ... 154
VII Water Quality Classes for Hydroponics ... 155
VIII Frequently Asked Questions of Hydroponics ... 156

GLOSSARY ... 164

REFERENCES ... 180

SUBJECT INDEX ... 183

CHAPTER 1

INTRODUCTION

Soil is the best available growing medium for the plants which provides anchorage, nutrients, air, water, etc. for successful plant growth. Soil is simply the holder of the nutrients, a place where the plant roots traditionally live and the base of support for the plant structure. Sometime, soil poses a serious limitation for plant growth due to presence of disease organisms & nematodes, unsuitable soil reaction, unfavourable soil compaction, poor drainage and degradation due to erosion, etc. On other hand, continuous cultivation of crops has resulted in poor soil fertility, which in turn has reduced the opportunities for natural soil fertility build up by microbes. This situation has lead to poor yield and quality. The Open Field Agriculture involves large space, lot of labour and large volume of water. In some places like metropolitan cities, soil is not available for crop growing. In such situations, hydroponics is an advantageous technology of gardening over the conventional growing procedures.

More recent successful methods of soil-less growth differ in particulars but have two common features: (1) nutrients are supplied in liquid solutions; and (2) plants are supported by porous material, such as peat, sand, gravel, or glass wool, that acts as a "wick" in relaying the nutrient solution from its source to the roots.

DEFINITION OF HYDROPONICS

In the early 1930's, **W. E. Gericke**, of the University of California, put laboratory experiments in plant nutrient solution on a commercial scale. In doing so, he termed these nutri-culture systems as **hydroponics.** The word was derived from two Greek words i.e., hydro, meaning water, and ponos, meaning labor, or literally, water working. **Gericke's** application of hydroponics soon proved itself by providing food for troops stationed on non-arable islands in the Pacific in the early 1940's. In 1945 the U.S. Air Force solved its problem of providing its personnel with fresh vegetables by practicing hydroponics on a large scale on the rocky islands normally incapable of producing such crops. With the development of plastics, hydroponics took another large step forward and is now a widely accepted method of producing certain specialty crops such as tomatoes, lettuce, cucumbers, and peppers. Other crops that can be grown by this method include herbs, foliage plants, and flowers. Most of the roses exported from Holland are grown hydroponically.

Hydroponics by definition means *water-working*. In practical use, it means growing plants in a water and nutrient solution, without soil. Hydroponics allows a gardener to grow plants in a more efficient and productive manner with less labour and time required. The science of hydroponics proves that soil is not required for plant growth but the elements, minerals and nutrients that soil contains are essential. Soil is simply the holder of the nutrients, a place where the plant roots traditionally live and a base of support for the plant structure.

The definition of hydroponics has gradually been broadened. Today it is used to describe all ways of growing plants without soil. It is synonymous with the term soil-less culture, and both terms are restricted to the growing of plants without soil.

Hydroponics is an advantageous method of gardening both for home and commercial use. Commercial growers have adopted these techniques to produce crops in circumstances that would otherwise be unfavourable. There are no weeds to deal with, and hydroponic plants are typically more healthy, mature earlier, and use less space.

With hydroponics the plants are grown in an inert growing medium, the plants do not get anything from the growing medium. The plants receive only what you give them, nothing more, you have complete control over pH, nutrients and the nutrient strength. In the soil you really have no idea what the plants are getting, so gardening becomes a big guessing game. How much nutrient does the soil contain? What about the essential micro-nutrients should I fertilize? How much do I apply? How much of what I applied was washed away by the last watering or rain storm? The questions go on and on. Unless you have a very expensive soil analysis lab, you just don't know, you have to guess.

In hydroponics you provide the exact nutrients as per plants need, so they can develop and grow. The nutrients are fed directly at the root base, never stressing the plant due to lack of nutrients or water.

Virtually, any plant can be grown hydroponically, but some plants perform better than others. Hydroponic growing is ideal for fruit bearing crops such as tomatoes, cucumbers and peppers, leafy crops like lettuce and herbs and flowering plants.

In combination with greenhouses, it is high technology and capital-intensive. It is also highly productive, conservative of water and land, and protective of the environment. Yet for most of its employees, hydroponic culture requires only basic agriculture skills. Since regulating the aerial and root environment is a major concern in such agricultural systems, production takes place inside enclosures designed to control air and root temperatures, light, water, plant nutrition, and adverse climate.

Most commercial hydroponic growers combine hydroponic technology with a controlled environment to achieve the highest quality produce. Within a green- house structure you can control the ambient temperature, humidity and light levels allowing you to grow on a year- round basis

The term hydroponics is used to describe many different types of systems for growing plants without soil. The most common systems are:

1. Water culture, aquaculture or nutriculture, a system of plant growing in which the plant roots are immersed in water containing dissolved nutrients.

2. Aggregate culture, A system of plant growing in which a material such as sand, gravel, or marbles supports the plant roots

3. Aeroponics A system of plant growing in which the plant roots hang in the air and are misted regularly with a nutrient solution
4. Continuous flow systems, a system of plant growing in which the nutrient solution flows constantly over the plant roots. This system is the one most commonly used for commercial production.

Fig. 1.1: Hydroponic culture of lettuces.

There are many types of controlled environment / hydroponic systems. Each component of controlled-environment agriculture (CEA) is of equal importance, whether it be the structural design, the environmental control, or the growing system. Not every system is cost-effective in every location. All too often, importance is given to only one or two of the key components, but the system fails due to lack of attention to any one of the components. If improper attention is given to the greenhouse structure and its environment, no hydroponic system will prove economically viable. While hydroponic and CEA are not synonymous, CEA usually accompanies hydroponics. Their potentials and problems are inextricable.

WHY DO PEOPLE PREFER HYDROPONICS?

Hydroponic gardening is an easy, environmentally sound way to grow a wide variety of healthy plants. It offers numerous benefits including:

- Plants grow up to 50% faster than in soil because they have easy access to food and water.

- Plants become "vacation-proof" and "neglect-resistant".
- Nutrients are directly available to plants and don't get bound up.
- Little or no pesticides are necessary. Plants start out in a disease-free medium.
- Smaller containers can be used because the roots can grow without being root bound.
- Gardening is possible where it would not be normally e.g. poor soil, rocky areas, even balconies. With the use of artificial lighting it is even possible to successfully garden in a spare room or garage.
- Less labor is required than growing in soil because no digging or weeding is required.
- Since plants do not need to compete for nutrients, more can be grown in a smaller area.
- The increased control over growing conditions makes it easier to provide the best possible environment for plants, leading to better quality produce and higher yields.
- Fast growing healthy plants grown by hydroponic methods are more resistant to pests and diseases.
- You will also notice improved flavor and texture in hydroponically grown fruit and veggies.

CHAPTER 2

HISTORY OF HYDROPONICS

Hydroponic systems have been used for centuries. Hydroponics is at least as ancient as the pyramids in Egypt. It is believed that hydroponics started in the ancient city of Babylon with its famous hanging gardens, which was listed as one of the Seven Wonders of the Ancient World. This was probably one of the first successful attempts to grow plants hydroponically. Ancient Egyptian hieroglyphic records dating back to several hundred years B.C. describe the growing of plants in water along the Nile River without soil. Before the time of **Aristotle, Theophrastus (325-287 B.C.)** undertook various experiments in crop nutrition.

Hydroponic was described by **Marco Polo** in his famous journals. As he traveled through China (c1275 -c1292), he wrote of the floating gardens of the Chinese.

The earliest record of scientific approach to discover plant constitutes was in 1600. This is when Belgian **Jan van Helmont** showed in his classical experiment that plants obtain substances from water. He planted a 5-pound willow shoot in a tube containing 200 pounds of dry soil that was covered to keep the dust out. He left it for five years and watered it regularly from rain water. His results were that the willow shoots increased weight by 160 pounds, while the soil lost almost 2 ounces. It was European plant physiologists that established plants absorb water through plant roots that pass through the plant stem. They showed that the roots of plants absorb minerals from soil and water.

The first recoded experiments were conducted in England in 1699 by **John Woodward,** a fellow of the Royal Society of England. The plants of spearmint were grown in water containing various amounts of soil by **Mr. Woodward** and he found that the better growth occurred in the water which contained small amount of soil or suspended solids. He concluded that plant growth was a result of certain substances and minerals in the water, derived from the soil. This mixture of water and soil was the first man-made hydroponic nutrient solution.

European plant physiologists established many things in the decades that followed **Woodward's** research. They proved that water is absorbed by plant roots, that it passes through the plants stem system and that it escapes into the air through pores in the leaves. They also showed that plant roots take up minerals from either soil or water and that leaves draw carbon dioxide from the air. They also demonstrated that plant roots take up oxygen.

In 1792, English scientist **Joseph Priestly** discovered that plants placed in a chamber filled with carbon dioxide will gradually absorb the carbon dioxide and give off oxygen. Two years later, **Jean Ingen-Housz** demonstrated that plants in a chamber filled with carbon dioxide could replace the gas with oxygen within several hours if the chamber was placed in sunlight. It was a fact that the plant was responsible for this transformation, eluding to the first concept of photosynthesis.

From discoveries and developments in the years 1859-1865, this technique was accomplished by two German scientists, **Julius von Sachs** (1860), professor of Botany at the University of Wurzburg (1832-1897), and **W. Knop** (1861), an agricultural chemist. **Knop** has been called "The Father of Water Culture." In the same year, **Professor Julius von Sachs** published the first standard formula for a nutrient solution that could be dissolved in water where plants could grow through that technique. The name given to this technique was nutriculture which is still used in laboratory today. Finally, due to **von Sachs** efforts, the source to essential nutrients of growing plants was discovered. However, the solution was solely based on research rather than crop production.

In the early 1930's, **W. E. Gericke**, of the University of California, put laboratory experiments in plant nutrition on a commercial scale. In doing so, he termed these nutriculture systems as **hydroponics**. The word was derived from two Greek words, hydro, meaning water, and ponos, meaning labor, or literally, water working. **Gericke's** application of hydroponics soon proved itself by providing food for troops stationed on non-arable islands in the Pacific in the early 1940's. In 1945, the U.S. Air Force solved its problem of providing its personnel with fresh vegetables by practicing hydroponics on a large scale on the rocky islands normally incapable of producing such crops. With the development of plastics, hydroponics took another large step forward and is now a widely accepted method of producing certain specialty crops such as tomatoes, lettuce, cucumbers, and peppers. Other crops that can be grown by this method include herbs, foliage plants, and flowers. Most of the roses exported from Holland are grown hydroponically.

Dr. Gericke photographed the tomato plants that exceeded 25 ft. in length. These photographs appeared in newspapers throughout the country and created both excitement and skepticism in the general public. Promoters and equipment manufacturers proceeded to cash in on the media-hype by selling useless equipment and materials promoted to grow goliath plants. In reality, **Dr. Gericke's** newly developed hydroponic growing system was far too scientific and complex for most potential commercial growers.

His results were excellent, but very difficult to maintain by keeping a sufficient supply of oxygen in the nutrient solution. It was on Ascension Island that the first hydroponic farms were built. This is a small island in the South Atlantic where the Air Force stops and fuels. Since the island was completely barren they needed a way to grow fresh vegetables in order to provide the members with the nutrients they needed to be healthy. The successes that come from that island have now spread to other islands in the Pacific. **Dr. Gericke** is definitely the **father of Hydroponics.**

Between the early 1800's and the 1920's, phenomenal discoveries and developments were achieved in laboratory studies of plant physiology and plant nutrition. In 1925, the greenhouse industry expressed interested in the newly acquired knowledge in **Nutriculture**, as it was called at that time. Between 1925-1935, extensive development took place in converting the laboratory techniques of nutriculture to large-scale crop production.

Many would be hydroponic growers encountered problems with the Gericke system because it required a great deal of technical knowledge and ingenuity to build. Greicke's system consisted of a series of troughs or basins over which he stretched a fine wire mesh. This is turn was covered by a mulch of straw or other material. The plants were placed on this mesh, with the roots extending downward into a water / nutrient solution in the basin.

One of the main difficulties with this method was keeping a sufficient supply of oxygen in the nutrient solution. The plants would exhaust the oxygen rapidly, taking it up through the roots. For this reason, a continuous supply of fresh oxygen is imperative and be introduced into the solution through some methods of aeration. Another problem was supporting the plants so that the growing tips of the roots were held in the solution properly.

The American Press made their usual and many irrational claims, hailing it as the discovery of the century, in the most outlandish manner. After an unsettled period in which unscrupulous promoters tried to cash in on the idea by peddling useless equipment and material, more practical research was done and hydroponics soon became established on a sound scientific basis in horticulture with recognition of its two principal advantages, high crop yields and it's special utility in non-arable regions of the world.

In 1936, **W R Gericke** and **J R Travernetti** of the University of California published on account of the successful cultivation of tomatoes in a water and nutrient solution. Since then a number of commercial growers started experimenting with the techniques and researchers and agronomists at a number of agricultural colleges began working to simplify and perfect the procedures. Numerous hydroponic units, some on a very large scale, have been built in Mexico, Puerto Rico, Hawaii, Israel, Japan, India and Europe. In United States, without much public awareness, hydroponics has become big business, more than 500 hydroponic greenhouses have been started.

During the late 1940s **Robert B** and **Alice P Withrow**, working at Purdue University, developed a more practical hydroponic method. They used inert gravel as a rooting medium. By alternately flooding and draining the gravel in a container, plants were given maximum amounts of both nutrient solution and air to the roots. This method later became known as the gravel method of hydroponics, sometimes also termed nutriculture.

One of the first of several large hydroponics farms was built on Ascension Island in the South Atlantic. Ascension was used as a rest and fuel stop by the United States Air Force, and the island was completely barren. Since it was necessary to keep a large force there to service planes, all food had to be flown or shipped in. There was a critical need for fresh vegetables, and for this reason the first of many such hydroponic installations was established by armed forces there. The plants were grown in a gravel medium with the solution pumped into the gravel on a preset cycle. The techniques developed on Ascension were used in later installation on various islands in the Pacific such as Iwo Jima and Okinawa.

On Wake Island, west of Hawaii, normally incapable of producing crops, the rocky nature of the terrain ruled out conventional farming. The U.S Air Force constructed small hydroponic growing beds there that provided only 120 square feed of growing area. However, once the operation become productive, its weekly yield consisted of 30 pounds of tomatoes, 20 pounds of string beans, 40 pounds of sweet corn and 20 heats of lettuce.

The U.S Army also established hydroponic growing beds on the island of Iwo Jima that employed crushed volcanic rock as the growing medium, with comparable yields.

During the same period (1945), the Air Ministry of London took steps to commence soil-less culture at the desert base of Habbaniya in Iraq, and the arid island of Bahrain in the Persian Gulf, where important oil fields are situated. In the case of the Habbaniya, vital link in Allied communication, all vegetables had to be brought by air from Palestine to feed the troops stationed there, an expensive business.

Both the American Army and the Royal Air Force opened hydroponic units at military bases. Many millions of tons of vegetables produced without soil were eaten by Allied Soldiers and Airmen during the war years. After World War II the military command continued to use hydroponics. For example, The United States Army has a special hydroponics branch, which grew over 8,000,000 lbs of fresh produce during 1952, a peak year for military demand.

They also established one of the world's largest hydroponics installations, a 22 hectare project at Chofu, Japan. It became necessary to use hydroponics in Japan because of the method of fertilization of the soil by the Japanese.

It had been their practice for many years to use "Night Soil", containing human excreta as a fertilizer. The soil was highly contaminated with various types of bacteria and amoeba and although the Japanese were immune to these organisms, the occupying troops were not.

Covering 55 acres, it was designed to produce both seedlings and mature vegetables for American occupation forces. It remained in operation for over 15 years. The largest hydroponic installations up to that time were built in Japan using the gravel culture method. Some of the most successful installations have been those at isolated bases, notably in Guyana, Iwo Jima and Ascension Island.

After World War II, a number of commercial installations were built in the United States. The majority of these were located in Florida. Most were out of doors and subject to the rigours of the weather. Poor construction techniques and operating practices caused many of them to be unsuccessful and production inconsistent. However, the commercial use of hydroponics grew and expanded throughout the world in the 1950s to such countries as Italy, Spain, France, England, Germany, Sweden, the USSR and Israel.

One of the many problems encountered by the early hydroponics pioneers was caused by the concrete used for the growing beds. Lime and other elements leached into the nutrient solution. In addition, most metals were also affected by the various elements in the solution. In many of these early gardens, galvanized and iron pipe were used.

Not only did they corrode very quickly, but elements harmful or toxic to the plants were released into the nutrient solution.

Nevertheless, interest in hydroponic culture continued for several reasons. First, no soil was needed, and large plant population could be grown in a very small area. Second, when fed properly, optimum production could be obtained. With most vegetables, growth was accelerated and, as a rule, the quality was better than that of soil grown vegetables. Produce grown hydroponically had much longer shelf life of storage qualities.

Many of the oil and mining companies built large gardens at some of their installation in different parts of the world, where conventional farming methods were not feasible. Some were in desert areas with little or no rainfall or sub-surface waters, and other were on islands, such as those in Caribbean, with little or no soil suitable for vegetable production.

Big commercial American headquarters in the Far East have over 80 acres devoted to vegetable units, to feed landless city dwellers, while various oil companies in the West Indies, the Middle East, the sandy wastes of the Arabian Peninsula and the Sahara Desert, operating in barren areas, especially off the Venezuelan Coast at Aruba and Curacao and in Kuwait have found soil-less methods invaluable for ensuring that their employees get a regular ration of clean, heath-giving green-stuff.

In addition to the large commercial systems built between 1945 and the 1960s, much work was done on small units for apartments, homes and backyards, for growing both flowers and vegetables. Many of these were not a complete success because of a number of factors; Poor rooting media, the use of unsuitable materials, particularly in constructing the troughs used as growing beds and crude environmental control.

Even with the lack of success in many of these ventures, hydroponics growers convinced the world that their problems could be solved. There was also a growing conviction in the minds of many that the perfection of this method of growing food was absolutely essential in light of declining food production and the world-wide population explosion.

Recent surveys have indicated that there are over 1,000,000 household soilless culture units operating in the United States for the production of food alone. Russia, France, Canada, South Africa, Holland, Japan, Australia and Germany are among other countries where hydroponics is receiving the attention it deserves. J.F. Gaudet Salvinia.

In addition to the work being done to develop hydroponic systems for the production of vegetables, however, between 1930 and 1960, similar work was being conducted to develop a system to produce livestock and poultry feed. Researchers had found that cereal grains could be grown very rapidly in this manner. Using grains such as barley, they proved that 5 pounds of seeds could be converted into 35 pounds of lush green feed in 7 days. When used as a supplement to normal ratio, the green feed was extremely beneficial for all types of animals and birds. In lactating animals, milk flow was increased. In the feed lots, better conversion rates and grains were achieved at less cost per pound of grain. In breeding stock the potency of males and conception in females increased dramatically. Poultry also benefited in many ways. Egg production increased while cannibalism, a constant problem for poultry men, ceased.

Here again, however, in developing a system that would produce consistently, a number of problems arose. The early systems hat little or no environmental control, and with no control of temperature or humidity, there was a constant fluctuation in the growth rate. Mold and fungi in the grasses were in ever-present problem. The use of thoroughly clean seed grain with a high germination ratio was found to be absolutely essential if a good growth rate was to be achieved.

Nevertheless, in the face of these and other obstacles, a few dedicated researchers continued to work to perfect a system that could produce this nutritious feed continuously. With the development of new techniques, equipment and materials, units become available that were virtually trouble free. Many of these are in use today on ranches, farms, and in zoos all over the world.

HISTORICAL HIGHLIGHTS

- **1699: Woodward** in England found he could grow plants in water to which soil was added. 1850s **Liebig,** a German scientist, showed the value of the nutrient solution to study the nutritional requirements of plants. 1860s **Sach and Knop** of Germany prepared nutrient solutions from mineral salts, thus freeing plants from the need of soil for growth.
- **1870-1920s:** There was a gradual increase in knowledge regarding the nutrient requirements of plants.
- **1929: Professor Gericke** of California developed the first commercial hydroponic unit. He grew tomatoes in water culture which aroused much public interest, but enthusiasm waned as problems appeared, such as aeration and iron deficiency.
- **1936:** In the U.S.A., gravel culture for commercial crop production was developed.
- **1938:** Hoagland and Arnon of the University of California at **Berkeley** developed a nutrient solution which today is widely used in scientific fields and is known as Hoaglands solution.
- **1939-1945:** American forces on the remote and barren Ascension Island grew vegetable crops hydroponically. The system used was the Nutri-cultural system, developed at Purdue University by **Robert and Alice Withrow**. Gravel was the growing media, and the nutrient solution was made according to the Nutriculturely specifications.
- **1946-1970:** Initially producing in excess of 40 tons of fresh vegetables hydroponically, the U.S. Army constructed the worlds largest hydroponic farm on Chofu Island, Japan (26 x 90 meter-long gravel beds). Many hydroponic farms developed in the southern states of the U.S.A. where climatic extremes and shortage of land hindered the development of normal agricultural practice.
- **1970-1985:** This period witnessed the development of the Nutrient Film Technique and rockwool culture. There has been a sharp rise in world interest for the communal production of vegetables and flower crops. For example, Jersey Channel Islands,

in 1979, had six hectares under NFT, increasing rapidly in the 1980s. Cultivation by rockwool culture in the Netherlands has increased from about a half-hectare in 1975, to between 20-25 hectares in 1978, to over 1300 hectares in 1983. Expansion is continuing worldwide.

- **1990-onward:** Aeroponic and aquaculture systems lead the way in research, with genetically engineered plants now a reality. Insect control is now done with predator insects, pheromones, and fungal diseases for the bad insects. Research on hormones and auxins has resulted in the mass production of plants using tissue culture techniques.

CHAPTER 3

PRESENT STATUS AND FUTURE PROSPECTS OF HYDROPONICS

PRESENT STATUS

Although hydroponics has been around for many years, it is still a young science which has progressed quickly within the past forty years. Hydroponics has been adapted to many situations from outdoor farming to greenhouse and now in-home gardening.

United States of America is behind in the hydroponic technology but advancing. Western Europe and Canada extensively use hydroponics for commercial food products and, currently the Dutch are the recognized world leaders in commercial hydroponics. Holland has a total hydroponic production area of about 10,000 ha. China is growing 2,000 acres annually.

Hydroponics may be used in underdeveloped countries for food production in limited space. It is even feasible to grow hydroponically in areas of poor soil conditions such as deserts. The desert sand serves as a good growing media and seawater can be used to mix nutrient solution once the salts have been removed.

The popularity of Hydroponics has increased dramatically in a short period of time. Experimentation and research in the area of indoor and outdoor hydroponic gardening is an ongoing process. NASA has started to experiment with growing plants in space. Currently, plans are being drawn for using the techniques of soil-less culture on space flights and even on the moon, or beyond. Hydroponics is the wave of the future

Among the well-known institutions which have contributed so much to the establishment of the soil-less cultivation of plants as a practical proposition are, the Universities of Illinois, Ohio, Purdue and California in the United States; The University of Reading, in Great Britain, is famous for its pioneering work in new cropping techniques; Canada's Central Experimental Farm at Ottawa, as well as the internationally famous and important firm of Imperial Chemical Industries Ltd., which undertook the adoption of hydroponics to British conditions.

Other pioneers of hydroponics were the Boyce Thompson Institute for Plant Research, New York; the New Jersey Agriculture Experiment Station; the Alabama Polytechnic Institute, and the Horticultural Experiment Station, Naaldwijk, Netherlands.

In India, the author of this book has a major contribution in hydroponics. He started experiments in this field in 1992 and now has wide experience of practical hydroponics. Based on the findings of his work and long experience, the breakthrough in hydroponics was brought in after the development of a nutrient solution named as **bioplantomin.** This solution is balanced and complete food for the plants which can be used in growing a wide range of plant species under varied agro-climatic conditions in India. By using this solution in hydroponics, addition of other nutrients is not required. This solution is being sold by Indian Medicinal Plants Marketing Federation throughout India.

Currently the US has corporate hydroponic farms that cover as many as 60 acres and produce large quantities of hydroponic produce. Often this produce is shipped throughout the US. In addition, there are thousands of smaller hydroponic farms that cover 1/8 to 1 acre that usually grow premium hydroponic produce and market it in their local area. The most common hydroponic crop grown in the US is tomatoes, followed by cucumbers, lettuce, herbs, peppers and flowers.

The demand for premium produce is so high in the US that the number of current hydroponic farms cannot meet the demand. Every day hundreds to thousand pounds of hydroponic tomatoes, peppers and cucumbers are flown in from Canada, Europe and Mexico.

World wide, hydroponics has become a well established technology. In arid regions, such as Mexico and the Middle East, India and Israel, hydroponic culture is helping to feed growing populations. Nearly every country in the world uses hydroponic culture on some scale. In some cases, hydroponic produce is strictly considered a premium or gourmet product. In others, hydroponic technology is utilized for producing staple crops and grain. Hydroponic technology is even used by some zoos for producing animal feed.

The US Navy is growing fresh vegetables on submarines in highly specialized recirculating hydroponic systems to help supply fresh vegetables for the crews.

NASA is experimenting with recirculating hydroponic systems to be used to feed people in space. Many experiments have been conducted in laboratories and on recent space shuttle missions.

With today's technology, a small hydroponic grower with just 5,500 square ft. of greenhouse space (that's 1/8th of an acre) can grow as much as 50,000 pounds of hydroponic tomatoes annually.

As a concept, hydroponics has been around since the beginning of time. As a science, it is quite new. Hydroponics has only been used in commercial production for approximately 50 years. In that time, it has been applied to both indoor and outdoor farms, to growing premium produce, to feeding third world countries and to applications in the space program.

FUTURE PROSPECTS OF HYDROPONICS

Hydroponics is a very young science. It has been used on a commercial basis for only 40 years. However, even in this relatively short period of time, it has been adapted to many situations, from outdoor field culture and indoor greenhouse culture to highly specialized culture in atomic submarines to grow fresh vegetable for crews. It is a space age science, but at the same time can be used in developing countries of the Third World to provide intensive food production in a limited area. It's only restraints are sources of fresh water and nutrients. In areas where fresh water is not available, hydroponics can use seawater through desalination. Therefore, it has potential application in providing food in areas having vast regions of non-arable land, such as deserts. Hydroponic complexes can be located along coastal regions in combination with petroleum-fueled or atomic desalination units, using the beach sand as the medium for growing the plants.

Another area in which hydroponics promises to play an important role in the future is growing seedlings for reforestation, orchards, and ornamental shrubbery. In a report published in 1966, researchers at the University of Wisconsin stated that seedlings of white cedar, blue and white spruce, red pine, and others were grown in a controlled environment. Using a hydroponic system with controlled feedings of a nutrient solution, the results of growth in one year were three to four times as great as in year old nursery grown seedlings. The extension of the growing season in this northern area, through the use of hydroponics and more concentrated use of space, made it possible to grow five to ten times a many plants in a given area. Some plantings of pine were 18 years old at the time this report was published and were said to be growing vigorously. **Report - American Nursery Man, 1966.**

Hydroponics is a valuable means of growing fresh vegetables not only in countries having little arable land and in those which are very small in area yet have a large population. It could be particularly useful in some smaller countries whose chief industry is tourism. In such countries, tourist facilities, such as hotels, have often taken over most arable areas of the country, forcing local agriculture out of existence. Hydroponics could be used on the remaining non-arable land to provide sufficient fresh vegetables for the indigenous population as well as the tourists. Typical examples of such regions are the West Indies and Hawaii, which have a large tourist industry and very little farm land in vegetable production.

But there continues to be problems that hamper the growth and development of hydroponics as a whole. One problem is the negative attitude of the directors and people of position in many of our colleges, universities and government agencies, which has ranged from complete disinterest, to open hostility. This attitude partly results from their own failure to achieve crop yields matching those of many hydroponic growers.

Fortunately, in some of our schools, there are people who not only have open minds, but who have also given generously of their time and talents to help growers establish very successful hydroponic farms.

Another problem that has developed in the past few years is the ever-increasing cost of energy for heating. In many areas the high cost of fuel has caused a number of installations that were operating at a profit to suddenly plunge deeply into the red, and some operators have been forced to shut down entirely in the colder months. Since this is the time of year when vegetables are at or near peak prices, these increased fuel costs have had a disastrous effect on the industry as a whole, including soil-based greenhouse men.

One bright spot in this picture is the development of solar heating systems. Much research has and is being done in this field, and there are many ready-built systems available on the market today. Also available are a number of publications with detailed plans on how to build one's own solar energy system. There will of course, be many new developments in this field over the next few years, and solar energy may eventually solve the dilemma for all growers.

Currently, plans are being drawn for using the techniques of soil-less culture on space flights and even on the moon, or beyond. For hydroponics, the future seems very bright.

The biggest danger to the growth and development of hydroponics has been the influx of "instant experts" over the past 10 years. The success of many growers using properly designed equipment has attracted these self-styled authorities in ever-growing numbers. Making extravagant claims, they have sold many shabby, poorly made copies of workable units with the assurance that this was the easy road to riches. Many of these fly-by-night promotions have been short lived, but, sadly, others continue to flourish.

The cost to the would-be commercial grower for a properly designed hydroponic system, housed in a manner that provides good environmental control, can run into thousands of dollars. For this reason, he should check very closely the qualifications of the seller. He should require proof of claims regarding production and profit capability, back-up service after the sale, research facilities and past records of the manufacturing company.

If a person is willing to work and apply himself, plants can be grown hydroponically by a complete novice with no past experience at growing crops. The owner of a small 10 x 12 foot hydroponic greenhouse will be able to produce all the fresh vegetables needed by a family of four or five, provided he operates the unit on a year round basis.

Hydroponics can also be profitable on a commercial scale if the grower devotes the time and attention required for any successful business. The average yield of tomatoes per acre is eighteen times greater than in conventional soil methods. Rarely do pesticides have to be used.

As the technology is refined, hydroponics may become even more productive, feeding people around the world or even in space. Other areas where hydroponics could be used in the future include growing seedlings for reforestation, establishing orchards, growing ornamental crops, flowers and shrubs and integration with aquaculture, where the wastes provides nutrients to the plants and the plants help to purify the water the fish are living in.

MODERN HYDROPONICS

- The recent developments in plastics have cut hydroponic system costs which have made hydroponics financially feasible the more people.
- The development of pumps has allowed hydroponic systems to evolve to fully automatic systems.
- Presently, advances are being made in the development of highly specialized hydroponic cultures for use in atomic submarines.

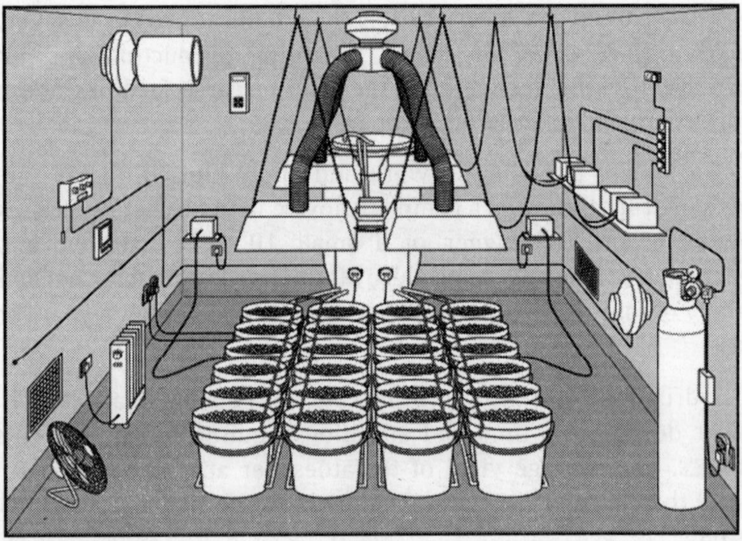

FUTURE STRATEGY OF HYDROPONICS

- Further development of the application of solar heating in hydroponic greenhouses will reduce cost and economic impact of hydroponics.
- Currently, plans are being drawn for using the techniques of soil-less culture on space stations, and perhaps one day on surfaces of other celestial bodies (planets, moons, etc.) that don't have soil.
- Developing countries, along with all other nations, will be able to feed many people using less land than current farming techniques.
- Advances in lighting technology will lead to a more widespread use of hydroponics in areas with limited seasonal sunlight.
- The application of hydroponics in providing food in areas having vast regions of non-arable land, such as deserts and mountainous terrain, will be more heavily used.

CHAPTER 4

ADVANTAGE AND LIMITATIONS OF HYDROPONICS

Hydroponics is probably the most intensive and fascinating method of crop production in today's agricultural industry. In combination with greenhouses and protective covers (controlled environment agriculture), it is high technology and capital intensive. With the possibility of adjusting air and root temperature, light, water, plant nutrition, and adverse climate, this combination can be made highly productive, conservative of water and land and protective of the environment.

The growing of plants hydroponically has number of advantages over open field agriculture. High-density maximum crop yield, crop production where no suitable land exists, crop cultivation regardless of seasonality, more efficient use of water and fertilizers and minimal use of land area are the principal advantages of hydroponics in combination with controlled environment agriculture. Another major benefit is the possibility of obtaining pesticide free products, which fetch higher prices at the increasingly ready markets, at present.

The important advantages of hydroponics are given below:

ADVANTAGES OF HYDROPONICS

1. The increased control over growing conditions makes it easier to provide the best possible environment for plants, leading to better quality produce and higher yields.

2. The production in hydroponics may be increased approximately two times as compared with soil cultivation in a comparable area with correct management practices because plants do not have to compete for moisture and nutrients
3. Hydroponic gardening can provide plants with optimum quantities of the necessary nutrients during the different seasons. This will enable maximum growth to be achieved.
4. A small hydroponic garden can be setup almost anywhere even in upstairs or balconies, open spaces and in protected structures because land is not necessary.
5. The work involved in hydroponics is generally light. Heavy manual operations associated with normal cultivation practices such as digging, making beds, watering, weeding and ploughing are eliminated.
6. Hydroponic produce generally tastes better and is higher in nutritional value than field grown crops.
7. Plants grow 50% faster than the soil grown under the same conditions because they have easy access to food and water.
8. Continuous cultivation and off-season production is possible
9. Occurrence of soil borne diseases or nematode damage is not possible, so hydroponic products are exported safely.
10. Vegetable cultivation can be done with leisure sense.
11. Many plants were found to give yield early in hydroponics system.
12. Disabled people who are unfit for open field cultivation can adopt hydroponic systems in gardening as benches may be adopted to their requirements.
13. Easy to hire labour as hydroponic system is more attractive and easier than cultivation in soil.
14. No need of electricity, pumps, etc. for the non-circulating systems of solution culture.
15. Offer possibility of growing a wide variety of vegetable and flower crops including anthurium, marigolds, etc.

16. Water wastage is reduced to minimum.
17. There is no need of crop rotations as growing medium can be reused continuously or replaced.
18. The plants are uniform in growth and maturity.
19. Erosion of top soil is not even an issue since hydroponic gardening systems use no top soil. If agricultural trends continue to erode top soil and waste water, hydroponics may soon be our only solution.
20. Hydroponic plants require very little energy to find and breakdown food. The plants then use this saved energy to grow faster and to produce more yield.
21. Hydroponics is not subject to variable weather conditions and seasonal changes due to controlled environment. For example, frost won't be a setback anymore because temperature is controlled. Strong winds and rain will no longer destroy crops due to an enclosed surrounding. These factors ensure maximum production.

LIMITATIONS OF HYDROPONICS

1. Hydroponics requires higher initial capital expenditure. The expenditure is increased further when the soil-less culture is combined with controlled environment agriculture.
2. Hydroponic systems require high degree of management skills especially for solution preparation, maintenance of pH and EC, nutrient deficiency judgment and correction, ensuring aeration, maintenance of favourable condition inside protected structures, etc.
3. Considering the significantly high cost, the soil-less culture is limited to high value crops of the area.
4. A large-scale cultivator may have to purchase instruments to measure pH and EC of the nutrient solution.
5. Energy inputs are necessary to run the system.

6. Yields were found to decrease when temperature of the solution rises during warm periods.
7. The sharing of nutrient solutions can spread disease and pests a lot faster in water than soil. Since plants are grown so close together, an entire crop could be destroyed before it could be controlled.

Most of the gardeners think that hydroponics is not associated with biotechnology. Webster's dictionary defines biotechnology as biological science when applied especially in genetic engineering and recombinant DNA technology. Plants that are grown hydroponically have not been genetically altered by the additions of foreign genes to enhance a desired trait. Genetically modifying plants is an invasive process where hydroponics is not.

Hydroponics is not organic. Webster's dictionary defines organic as, relating to yielding or involving the use of food produced with the use of feed or fertilizer of plant or animal origin without employment of chemically formulated fertilizers, growth stimulants, antibiotics, or pesticides. Farmers believe organic means no pesticides or herbicides. The plant must grow naturally without using man made chemicals to control pests, weeds and diseases. Organic process feeds the soil and the soil feeds the plant. It is expected for plants to find the nutrients from the soil, assuming that the soil contains all essential nutrients. In hydroponics, the plant is fed directly without spending energy seeking nutrients with its root but rather just spends its energy growing.

CHAPTER 5

HYDROPONIC TECHNIQUES AND THEIR CLASSIFICATION

CLASSIFICATION

Hydroponic systems are generally classified as under:

1. **Open system:** A system of hydroponics in which nutrient solution, once delivered to the plant roots, is not reused.
2. **Closed system:** A system of hydroponics in which surplus solution is recovered, replenished and recycled.

On the basis of nature of media used, the hydroponic systems are classified as under:

1. **Liquid hydroponics:** A system of hydroponics in which liquid medium is used.
2. **Aggregate system:** A system of hydroponics in which a material such as sand, gravel or marbles is used to support the plant roots.
3. **Aeroponic system:** A system of hydroponics in which rockwool, net pots, vine clips or other devices are used to support the plant while its roots grow completely submerged in nutrient solution.

On the basis of movement of solution, the hydroponics systems are classified as under:

1. **Passive systems:** A system of hydroponics without using pump. The plant takes up nutrient through a fiberous wick from the pot

to the nutrient solution. The solution will generally help a bubbler to maintain proper oxygenation.

2. **Active systems:** A system of hydroponics in which nutrient solution moves actively using a pump.

Current hydroponic systems of cultivation can be classified as under:

1. Liquid hydroponics (Solution culture or aquaculture)
   a) Circulating methods (closed systems)
      i) Nutrient film technique (NFT)
      ii) Deep flow technique (DFT)
   b) Non-circulating methods (open systems)
      i) root dipping technique
      ii) Floating technique
      iii) Capillary action technique
2. Aggregate systems (Solid media culture): These can be open systems or closed systems.
   a) Hanging bag technique
   b) Grow bag technique
   c) Trench or trough technique
   d) Pot technique
3. Aeroponics
   a) Root mist technique
   b) Fog feed technique

HYDROPONIC TECHNIQUES

Different hydroponics systems have been described as under:

1. LIQUID HYDROPONICS

A. Circulatory Methods (Closed Systems)

a. Nutrient Film Technique - NFT

The nutrient film technique (NFT) was developed by **Dr. Allen Cooper** in England in 1970, to increase the year-round production of greenhouse crops. It has since been widely adopted in Western Europe (**Cooper 1988, Douglas 1976, Resh 1987**).

The Nutrient Film Technique or NFT system is an active recovery type hydroponic system. Again, using submersible pumps and reusing nutrient solutions. The NFT uses a reservoir with a submersible pump that pumps the nutrient solution into a grow-tube where the roots suspended. The grow-tube is at a slight downward angle so the nutrient solution runs over the roots and back into the reservoir. The nutrient solution flows over the roots up to 24 hours per day.

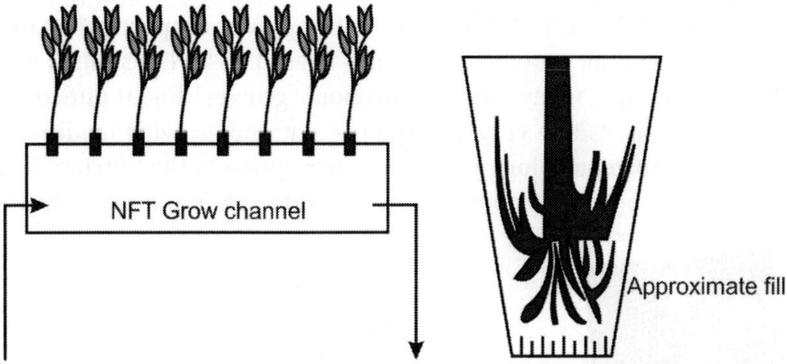

Fig. 5.1: Nutrient Film Technique.

In this method, no growing medium is required and the plants grow through light-proof plastic films placed over shallow, gently sloping channels. A steady flow of nutrients is maintained along the channel, and the roots grow into dense mats, with a thin film of nutrient passing over them (hence the name of the technique). A downside of the technique is that it has very little buffering against interruptions in the flow e.g. power outages, but overall, it is probably one of the more productive techniques.

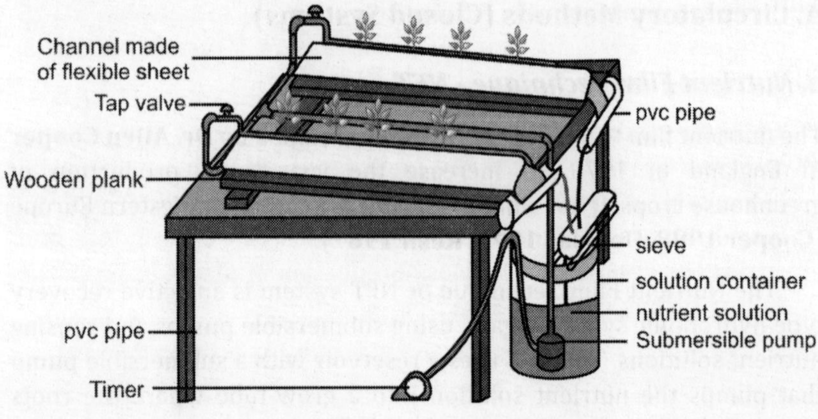

Fig. 5.2: Main features of NFT system.

Oxygen is needed in the grow-tube so capillary matting or air stones must be used. The plants are held up by a support collar or a grow-basket and no growing medium is used. The NFT system is very effective. Although, many novice hydroponic growers find it difficult to fine tune. It can also be very unforgiving, with no growing medium to hold any moisture, any long period of interruption in the nutrient flow can cause the roots to dry out and the plants to suffer and possibly die.

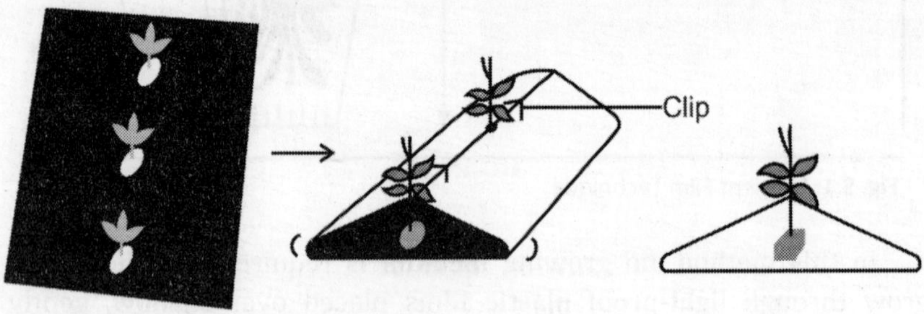

Fig. 5.3: Basic structure of NFT model.

Light must be prevented from reaching of the roots of the plants as this will prevent growth of the plants. It is important to check the nutrients level regularly. This can be minimized by replacing the nutrients solution on a regular basis.

A thin film of nutrient solution is always in contact with the roots. While the nutrient solutions circulated, the root surface is exposed to air. This helps the roots to breathe. This system is very good for producing fruits and vegetables.

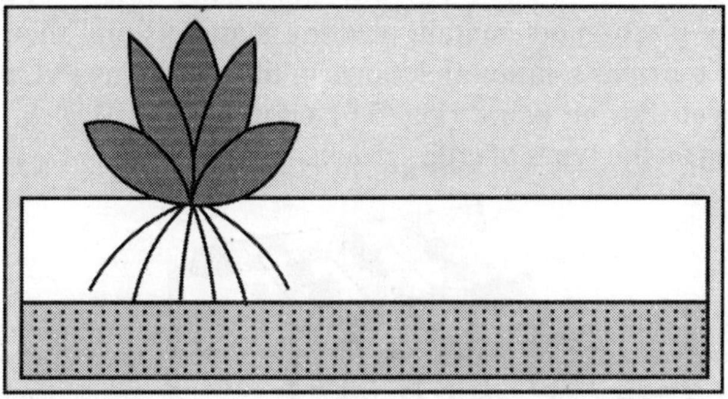

Fig. 5.4: Nutrient Film Technique – NFT.

b. Deep Flow Technique – DFT

A depth of nutrient solution (several inches deep) is circulated around the roots by a pump and gravity drain. This method is referred to as "Dynamic Root Floatation" or "Raceway Hydroponic" technique. This system is ideal for growing leafy vegetables.

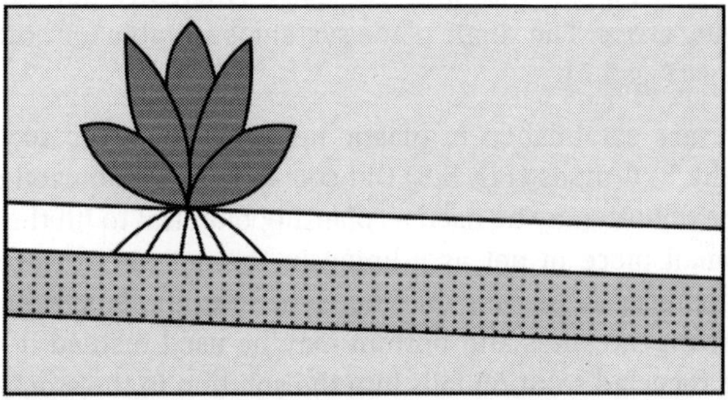

Fig. 5.5: Deep Flow Technique – DFT.

The deep flow technique (DFT) is a modified hydroponic culture method, which has been developed in Japan since 1973 specifically for the year-round production of Japanese honewort (*Cryptotaenia japonica* Hassk.) (**Ikeda 1984, 1985; Suzuki *et al.* 1984, Yamasaki 1986**).

As the name implies, 2-3 cm deep nutrient solution flows through 10 cm diameter PVC pipes to which plastic net pots with plants are fitted. The plastic pots contain planting materials and their bottoms touch the nutrient solution that flows in the pipes. The PVC pipes may be arranged in one plane (Fig. 5.6) or in zig zag (Fig. 5. 7) shape depending on the types of crops grown.

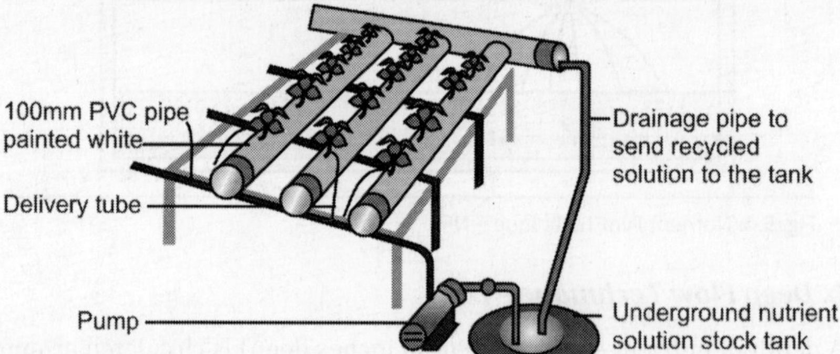

Fig. 5.6: Main features of Deep flow technique (Single plane pipe line system).

The zig zag system utilizes the space efficiently but suitable for low growing crops. The single plane system is suitable for both tall and short crops (Fig. 5.7).

Plants are established in plastic net pots and fixed to the holes made in the PVC pipes (Fig. 5.8) Old coir dust or carbonized rice husk or mixture of both may be used as planting material to fill the net pots. Place a small piece of net as a lining in the net pots to prevent the planting material falling into the nutrient solution. Small plastic cups with holes on the sides and bottom may be used instead of net pots. When the recycled solution falls into the solution in the stock tank, the nutrient solution gets aerated. The PVC pipes must have a slope of drop of 1 in 30-40 to facilitate the flow of nutrient solution. Painting the PVC pipes white will help reduce the heating up of nutrient solution. This system can be established in the open space or in protected structures as part of CEA.

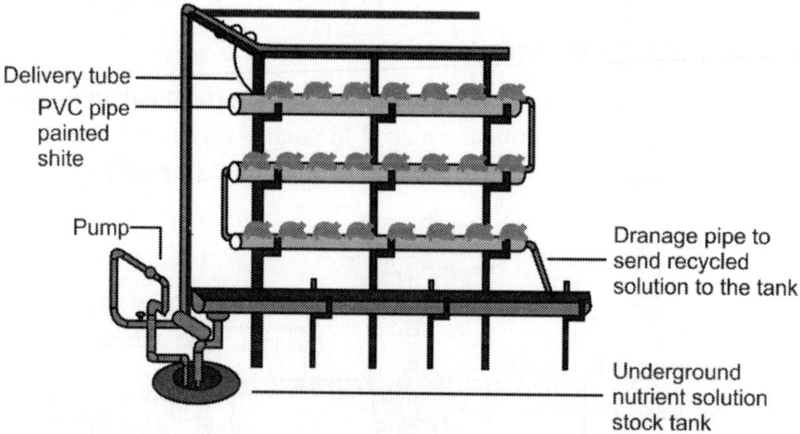

Fig. 5.7: Main features of Deep flow technique (Zig zag pipe system).

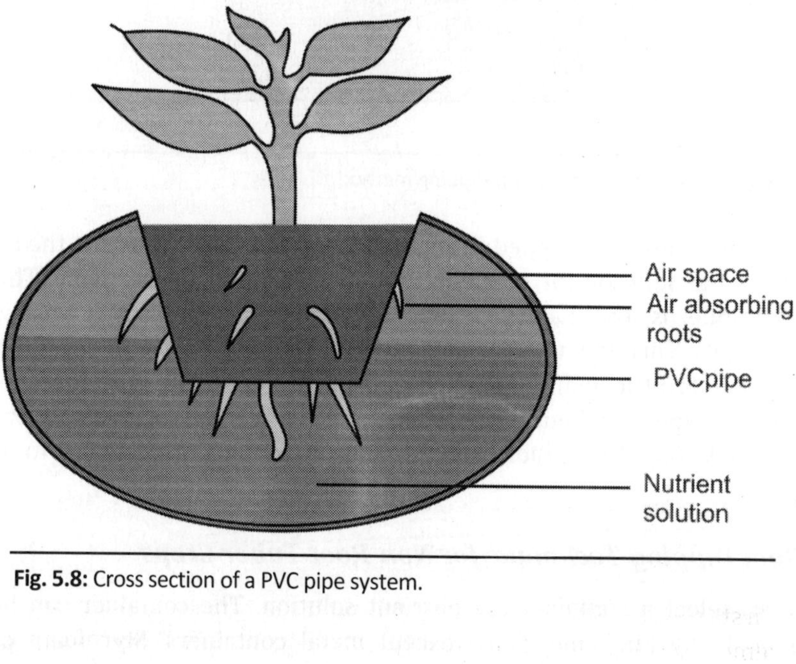

Fig. 5.8: Cross section of a PVC pipe system.

B. Non Circulating Methods (Open Systems)

The nutrient solution is not circulated but used only once. When its nutrient concentration decreases or pH or EC changes, it is replaced.

a. Root Dipping Technique

In this technique, plants are grown in small pots filled with little growing medium. The pots are placed in such a way that lower 2 – 3 cm of the pots is submerged in the nutrient solution (Fig 5.9).

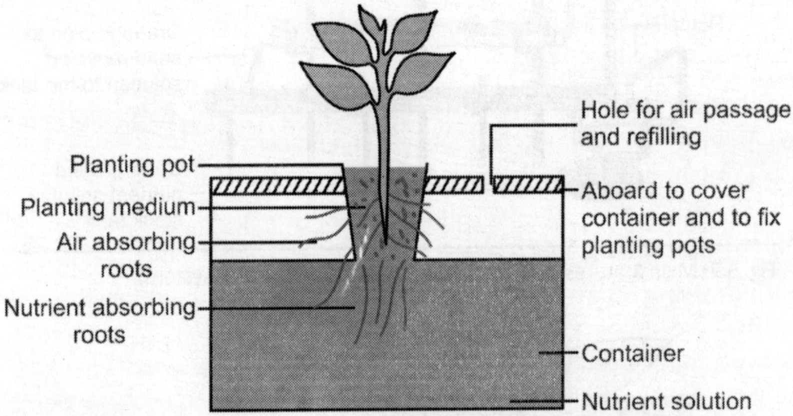

Fig. 5.9: Main features of root dipping method.

Some roots are dipped in the solution while others hang in the air above the solution for nutrient and air absorption, respectively. This technique is easy and can be developed using easily available materials. This 'low tech' growing method is inexpensive to construct and needs little maintenance. Importantly, this technique does not require expensive items such as electricity, water pump, channels, etc. For root crops (beet, radish, etc.) however, an inert medium has to be used.

Root Dipping Technique for Non-Root Tuber Crops

First, select a container for nutrient solution. The container can be almost any kind and shape except metal containers. Styrofoam or wooden boxes, plastic buckets or even cement troughs can be used. Styrofoam boxes are good as they can maintain the temperature of the nutrient solution. Place a black plastic sheet of at least 0.15 mm thickness as lining inside the boxes to avoid leakage and to reduce the light. The depth of the box must be about 25 - 30 cm to provide enough solution as well as enough space above the solution for oxygen absorbing roots.

A board is required to place on the container to prevent light penetration. The planting pots are also fixed to this board. The number of holes in the board to fix the pots depends on the crops to be grown. An additional hole is necessary for air circulation and refilling.

Seedlings are transplanted in plastic pots filled with sterilized old coir-dust or carbonized rice husk or the mixture of the two. Plastic net pots or plastic cups can be used. Make some holes at the bottom and on sides of the plastic cups for roots to emerge and for the nutrient solution to seep into the potting material. Place a small piece of net inside the pots or cups to prevent potting materials falling into the solution. Seeds could also be planted directly in the pots to raise the crop. Fill $2/3^{rd}$ of the container with nutrient solution. The pots with the plants are fitted on to the board and will be placed on top of the box. Only the bottom 2 cm of the pots will be submerged in nutrient solution. The above steps complete the formation of non-circulating hydroponic system. These boxes can be placed in net houses or in open space or under rain shelters or in-door. Tall growing plants will require some support to prevent from falling nutrient solution in the container. Success of the non-circulating hydroponic system depends on the rapid growth and quantity of roots that are exposed to the air. These roots absorb oxygen for the plants. Ideally, top two thirds of the young root system must be in the air and the rest must be floating / dipping in the nutrient solution. During crop growth, when the solution level in the container goes down, the ion concentration may increase. Such increase is detrimental to plant growth. If this condition is observed, siphon out the remaining solution and refill with fresh solution.

Root Dipping Technique for Root Tuber Crops

A 20 – 30 cm deep container can be used. It is lined with black polythene sheet and filled 1/3rd with nutrient solution. Leaving a space of about 7.5 cm above the solution level, fix a wire mesh in the box and fill with an inert medium. The seedlings / seeds are planted in the medium. At the early stage, nutrient solution will reach the planting medium through the perforated PVC pipe filled with the growing medium by capillary action. Later, plant roots will grow into the nutrient solution through wire mesh. At this stage, the perforated tube will be removed. The resulting hole will facilitate aeration and refilling.

b. Floating Technique

Float systems take advantage the surface of the nutrient solution. Most float systems are long, rectangular reservoirs built out of cement or wood and lined with a durable, poly liner. Holes are cut in a foam board which floats on the surface of the water and plants in net pots are set in the holes. The plant roots dangle in heavily aerated nutrient solution.

In areas where raw materials are limited and manufactured hydroponic systems and components are not available, the float system can be an economical means of hydroponic crop production.

c. Capillary Action Technique

Planting pots of different sizes and shapes with holes at the bottom are used. Fill these pots with an inert medium and plant seedlings / seeds in that inert medium. These pots are placed in shallow containers filled with the nutrient solution. Nutrient solution reaches inert medium by capillary action. Aeration is very important in this technique. Therefore, old coir dust mixed with sand or gravel can be used. This technique is suitable for growing ornamental flowers and indoor gardening.

2. AGGREGATE SYSTEMS

The following techniques involving inert solid media can be practiced using locally available materials. The media material selected must be flexible, friable, with water and air holding capacity and can be drained easily. In addition, it must be free of toxic substances, pests, disease causing microorganisms, nematodes, etc. The medium used must be thoroughly sterilized before use.

1. Inorganic natural media (gravel culture)
2. Organic natural media (smoked rice husk, saw dust, coconut fibre, coir dust and peat moss)
3. Inorganic artificial media (rockwool, perlite, vermiculite)
4. Organic artificial media (polyurethane, polyphenol, polyether, polyvinyl)

The most common types of media used in containerized systems of soil-less culture are peat-lite (**Boodley and Sheldrake** 1977), or a mixture of bark and wood chips. Tannins and acids present in the newly extracted coir-dust affect plants. Therefore, use at least 6 months old coir-dust. Dry, clean compressed coir-dust blocks are available for sale in the market. Different techniques described below, according to the method of holding the planting medium, can be practiced.

A. Hanging Bag Technique (Open System)

About 1 m long cylinder shaped, white (interior black) UV treated, thick polythene bags, filled with sterilized coconut fibre are used. These bags are sealed at the bottom end and tied to small PVC pipe at the top. These bags are suspended vertically from an overhead support above a nutrient solution-collecting channel. Therefore, this technique is also knows as 'verti-grow' technique. Seedlings or other planting materials established in net pots are squeezed into holes on the sides of the hanging bags. The nutrient solution is pumped to top of each hanging bag through a micro sprinkler attached inside the hanging bags at the top. This micro sprinkler evenly distributes the nutrient solution inside the hanging bag.

Nutrient solution drips down wetting the coconut fibre and plant roots. Excess solution gets collected in the channel below through holes made at the bottom of the hanging bags and flows back to the nutrient solution stock tank. This system can be established in the open space or in protected structures. In protected structures, the hanging bags in the rows and amongst the rows must be spaced in such a way that adequate sunlight falls on the bags in the inner rows.

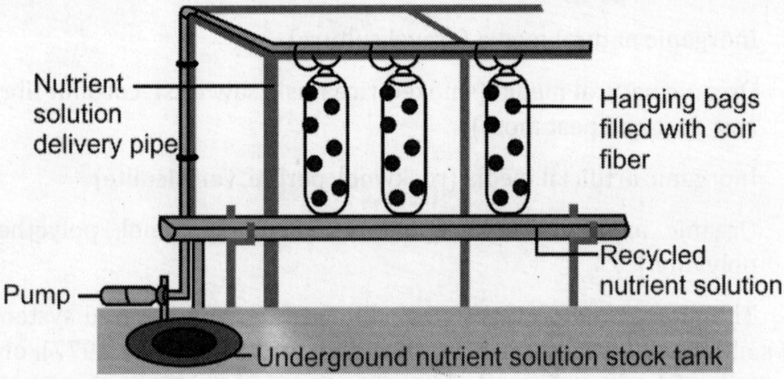

Fig. 5.10: Model of hanging bag technique.

The bags are not heavy as they are filled with coconut fibre and can be used for about 2 years. The number of plants per bag varies depending on the plants. About 20 lettuce plants can be established per bag. This system is suitable for leafy vegetables, strawberry, and small flower plants. Black colour tubes will have to be used for nutrient solution delivery to prevent mould growth inside.

B. Grow Bag Technique

Using grow bag is a simple and cheap way to grow plants hydroponically. In this technique, 1 – 1.5 m long white (inside black), UV resistant, polythene bags are used. These bags are about 6 cm in height and 18 cm wide. The bags are filled with growing medium of choice and open ends are sealed with freezer bag ties or insulation tape. These bags are placed end to end horizontally in rows on the floor with walking space in between. The bags may be placed in paired rows depending on the crop to grow. Polyethylene sheet may be placed underneath the bags to ensure good hygiene. Make small holes on the upper surface of the bags and squeeze seedlings or other planting materials established in net pots into the coir-dust. 2-3 plants can be established per bag. Make 2 small slits around the outside as edges of the bags approximately 10 mm from the base to allow drainage of excess nutrient solution. Lay-flat bags, which have drainage slits (or overflow ports) cut along the sides an inch (2. 54 cm) or so above the base, would also benefit from a protective plastic sheet beneath them. 4 to 6 plants per bag are usually recommended but the number will vary according to the type of plant grown or size of the bag.

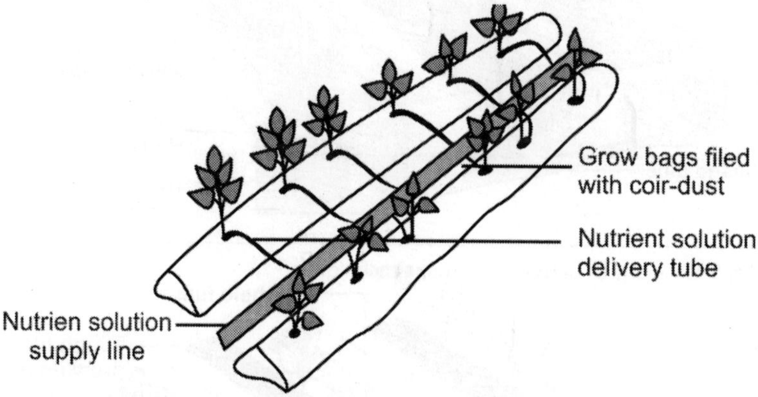

Fig. 5.11: Diagrammatic view of grow bag technique.

Fertigation with black capillary tube leading from main supply line to each plant is practiced. The nutrient solution and water may also be added manually to these bags. Depending on the stage of crop growth and the prevailing weather conditions, vary the amount of water applied. Make sure that the growing media is not completely saturated with water or nutrient solution, as it prevents the oxygen supply to plant roots. Cover the entire floor with white UV resistant polythene before placing the bags. This white polythene reflects the sunlight to the plants. It also reduces the relative humidity in between plants and incidence of fungal diseases. When tall growing plants are established supporting structures will be necessary.

C. Trench or Trough Technique

In this open system, plants are grown in narrow trenches in the ground or above ground troughs constructed with bricks or concrete blocks. Both trenches and troughs are lined with waterproof material (thick UV resistant polythene sheets in two layers) to separate the growing media from rest of the ground. The width of the trench or trough can be decided depending on the ease of operation. Wider trenches or troughs will permit two rows of plants.

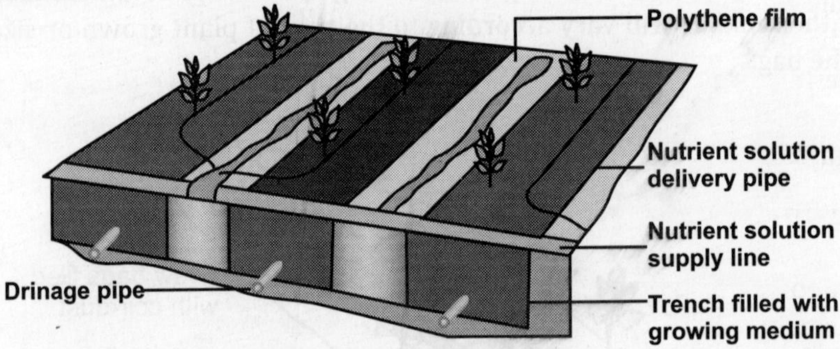

Fig. 5.12: Features of trench or trough technique.

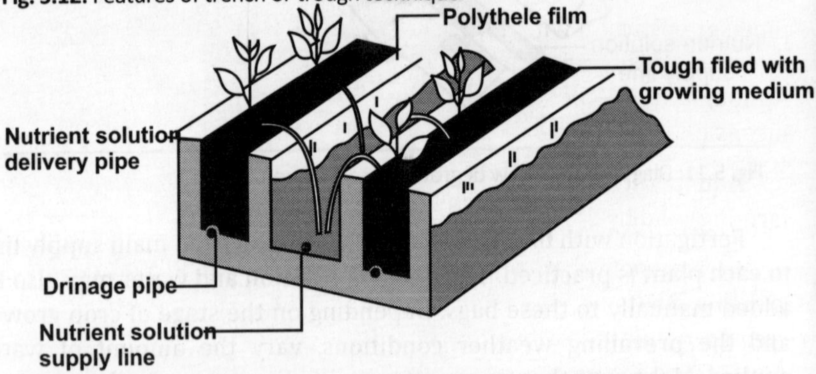

Fig. 5.13: Wholistic view of hydroponic trenches.

The depth varies depending on the plants to grow and a minimum of 30 cm may be necessary. Old coir dust, sand or gravel, peat, vermiculite, perlite, old sawdust or mixture of these materials can be used as the media for this culture. The nutrient solution and water are supplied through a drip irrigation system or manual application is also possible subject to labour availability. A well-perforated pipe of 2.5 cm diameter may be placed at the bottom of the trough or trench to drain out excess nutrient solution. Tall growing vine plants (cucumber, tomato, etc.) need additional support to withstand the weight of the fruits.

D. Pot Technique

Pot technique is similar to trench or trough culture but growing media is filled in clay or plastic pots. Volume of the container and growing media depend on the crop growth requirements. The volume ranges generally from 1 to 10 litres. Growing media, nutrient solution supply, providing support to plants, etc. is similar to that of trough or trench culture.

3. AEROPONICS

Aeroponics is the method of growing in which the plant roots are constantly misted with a nutrient solution. Designs include an A-frame with boards on each side, plant plugs set in each side and a mister between the boards spraying the roots. A round, large diameter PVC pipe set vertically with plant plugs all they way around and a mister mounted inside is another way to set up an aeroponic system. Although aeroponics is a unique way of growing, it is not a common means of commercial production.

Aquaponics is simply the combination of aquaculture (fish farming) and hydroponics (growing plants without soil).

In aquaponics, the fish waste provides a food source for the growing plants and the plants provide a natural filter for the fish. This creates a mini ecosystem where both plants and fish can thrive. Aquaponics is the ideal answer to a fish farmer having problem of disposing of nutrient rich water and a hydroponic growers need for nutrient rich water.

Commercially, aquaponics is in its infancy but, as the technology develops and is refined, it has the potential to be a more efficient and space saving method of growing fish, vegetables and herbs. By incorporating aquaponics, hydroponic growers can eliminate the cost and labor involved in mixing a fertilizer solution and commercial aquaculturists may be able to drastically reduce the amount of filtration needed in recirculating fish culture.

Although there are currently a limited number of commercial aquaponic operations, many people are expressing a strong interest in this intensive method of food production.

Although the practices of fish farming and soil-less plant culture have been traced to ancient times, the combination of the two is quite new. Research in aquaponics began in the 1970's and continues today. Several universities worldwide are dedicating resources to further the technology. At the University of the Virgin Islands, Dr. James Rakocy and his associates have developed a commercially viable aquaponics system designed for use in the tropics where natural fish populations have been depleted and most agricultural products must be imported.

Aeroponic systems have been described hereunder:

A. Root Mist Technique (RMT)

A mist of nutrient solution is sprayed every 4-5 minutes onto the roots of the plants that hang from a holding frame in a root chamber. This technique is popularly known as **Aeroponics**. This system is good for initiating rooting of cuttings and also for extracting (milking) phytochemicals from the roots for medicinal purposes.

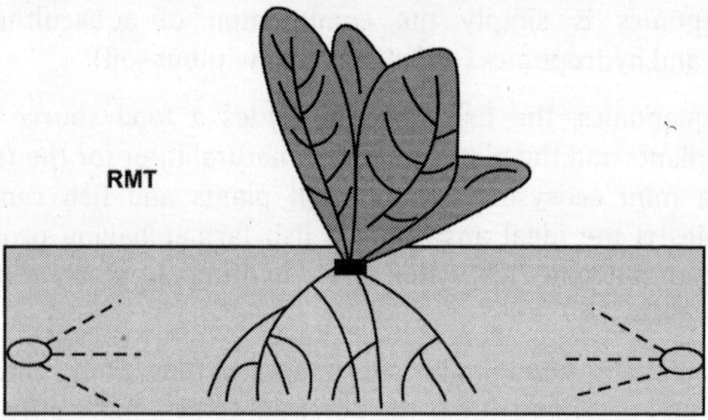

Fig. 5.14: Root Mist Technique (RMT).

B. Fog Feed Technique (FFT)

This is similar to RMT but the droplet size is so very minute that the nutrient solution can hardly moisten our hand. This technique has yet to be perfected. It is good for plants having aerial roots. e.g. orchids, anthuriums, etc.

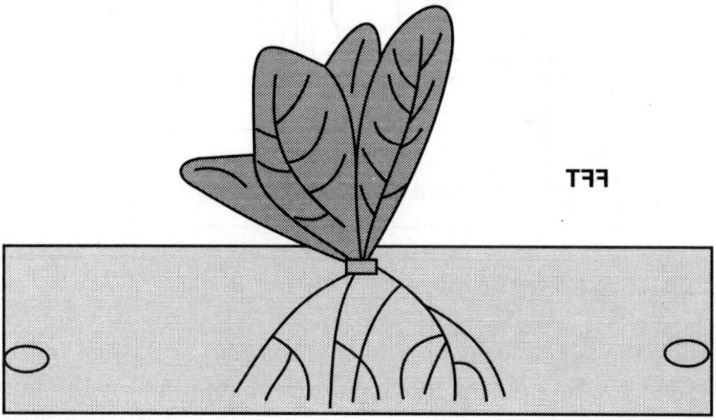

Fig. 5.15: Fog Feed Technique (FFT).

OTHER TECHNIQUES

1. The Ebb and Flow System

The Ebb and Flow hydroponic system is an active recovery type system. The Ebb and Flow uses a submersible pump in the reservoir and the plants are in the upper tray. They work on a simple flood and drain theory. The reservoir holds the nutrient solution and the pump. When the pump turns on, the nutrient solution is pumped up to the upper tray and delivered to the root system of the plants. The pump should remain on for about 20 to 30 minutes, which is called a flood cycle. Once the water has reached a set level, an overflow pipe or fitting allows the nutrient solution to drain back into the reservoir. The pump remains on for the entire flood cycle. After the flood cycle the nutrient solution slowly drains back down into the reservoir through the pump.

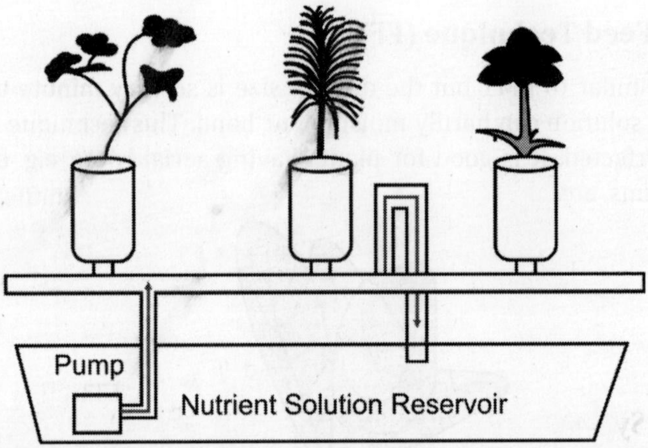

Fig. 5.16: Ebb and Flow type system.

During the flood cycle, air (poor in oxygen) is pushed out of the root system by the upward moving nutrient solution. As the nutrient solution drains back into the reservoir, oxygen rich air is pulled into the growing medium. This allows the roots ample oxygen to maximize their nutrient intake. Rockwool and grow rocks are most commonly used growing mediums in Ebb and Flow type systems. The Ebb and Flow is low maintenance, yet highly effective type of hydroponic gardening. This method is popular with many home hydroponic gardens and is ideal for growing a broad variety of crops since both long and short term crops do well in this system.

2. Drip System

The drip system is an active recovery or non-recovery type system. This system uses a submersible pump in a reservoir with supply lines going to each plant. With drip emitter for each plant the gardener can adjust the amount of solution per plant. A drip tray under each row of plants, sending the solution back to the reservoir, can easily make this system an active recovery type. In the early days of hydroponics, the extra solution was leached out into the ground. Drip systems are often used with Rockwool. Although, any growing medium can be used with this system, thanks to the adjustment feature on each individual drip emitter.

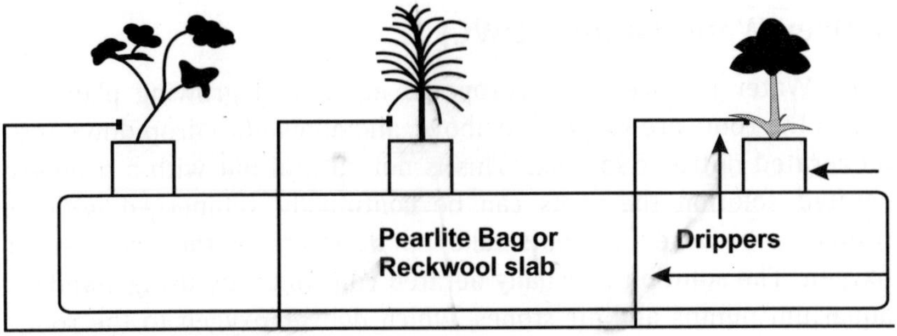

Fig. 5.17: Drip System.

3. Wick System

The wick system is a passive non-recovery type hydroponic system. It uses no pumps and has no moving parts. The nutrients are stored in the reservoir and moved into the root system by capillary action often using a candle or lantern wick. In simpler terms, the nutrient solution travels up the wick and into the root system of the plant. Wick systems often uses sand or perlite, vermiculite mix and a growing medium. The wick system is easy and inexpensive to set-up and maintain. Although, it tends to keep the growing medium to wet, which doesn't allow for the optimum amount of oxygen in the root system. The wick system is not the most effective way to garden hydroponically.

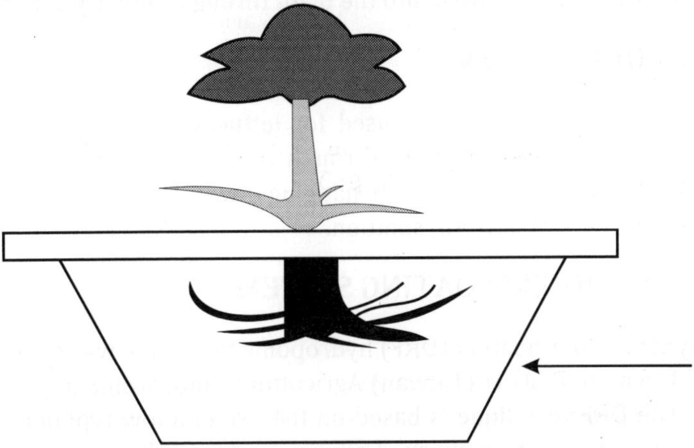

Fig. 5.18: Passive system.

4. Deep Water Culture (DWC)

Deep Water Culture is a hydroponic method of growing plants in which the roots are suspended above, and allowed to drop down into an aerated nutrient solution. This is not natural but with a properly aerated solution the roots can be continually submerged without problems because the roots take up nutrients in the presence of oxygen. The solution is usually aerated constantly by using standard aquarium pumps and air stones, which deliver oxygen to the roots. The container holding the roots and aerated nutrient solution must be completely light proof in order to prevent algae growth. The solution must be topped up from time to time.

DRIP FEEDING

Similar to Flood and Drain in its physical setup, except the pump delivers a continuous trickle of nutrients and water onto the medium. The emitters are commonly set to run 5 to 10 minutes every hour.

WICK FEEDING

A variation on Drip feeding, except that the plant draws water by means of a wick. The wick runs from the base of the plant container (e.g. a pot or a tray) down to a bottle of nutrient feed solution. The solution travels up the wick into the plant through capillary action.

RAFT CULTIVATION

A variant of DWC sometimes used for lettuces: sheets of expanded polystyrene have holes drilled through them, and young plants are placed in the holes with the roots hanging down. The sheet then floats in a shallow tank of nutrient solution.

DYNAMIC ROOT FLOATING SYSTEM

The dynamic root floating (DRF) hydroponic technique was developed at the Taichung District (Taiwan) Agricultural Improvement Station in 1986. The DRF technique is based on the use of a low typhoon-proof greenhouse with a framework of piping, a ridged culture bed, concave panels, an aspirator, a nutrient level adjuster, a nutrient exchange box and a nutrient concentration controller. Over the hot summer season, the DRF technique reduced the build-up of heat in the greenhouse, and induced plants to develop an aeroroot system to overcome the shortage of dissolved oxygen in the nutrient solution. There are now more than 19 ha of DRF hydroponic vegetable factories run by 150 growers in Taiwan, and another 0.6 ha in various parts of Thailand, Malaysia and Singapore.

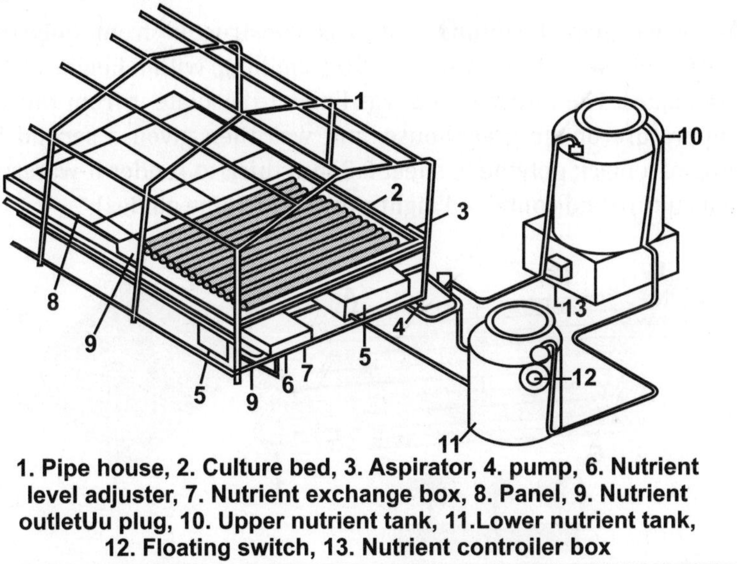

Fig. 5.19: 1. Pipe hours, 2. Culture bed, Aspirator, 4. Pump, 5. Reservoir, 6. Nutrient level adjuster, 7. Nutrient exchange box, 8. Panel, 9. Nutrient outlet plug, 10. Upper nutrient tank, 11. Lower nutrient tank, 12. Floating switch, 13. Nutrient controller box.

The DRF hydroponic system comprised a ridged culture bed, a concave panel, an aspirator, a nutrient level adjuster, a nutrient exchange box and a nutrient concentration controller, all of which were housed in a low, typhoon-proof greenhouse. The framework of the greenhouse was made of galvanized tubular iron piping 0.5°F and 0.75°F. The standard width of the house was 2.13 m, with a height of 2.1 m. The length of the house could be extended indefinitely, depending on the vegetable supply and the grower's production capacity. A dew-resistant transparent PVC plastic film 0.15-0.20 mm thick was lain on top of the greenhouse as a rainproof cover, while the sides were covered with a white polythene plastic net (24 mesh) to keep insects out. When the inside temperature was higher than 30°C, a black polythene plastic net (25-40% shading capacity) was hung 30 cm above the plastic house to reduce the build-up of heat in the greenhouse.

RIDGED CULTURE BED

The wave shaped culture unit was constructed from polystyrene board, and was 2.01 m wide and 90.1 cm long, with a height of 15 cm at the sides. The nutrient bed was lined, to insulate it from the inside temperature of the greenhouse, and was then given a second inner lining of a black polythene sheet 0.2 mm thick to render it waterproof. Each culture bed contained eight ridges (and nine gullies).

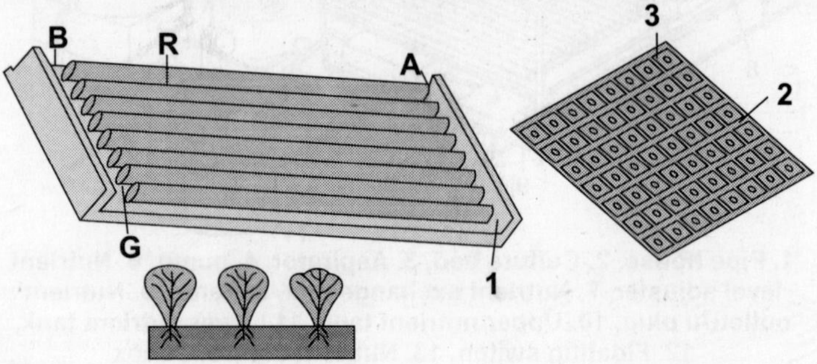

Fig. 5.20: The appearance of the ridged culture bed and concave panel.

Concave Panel

The panel shown in Fig. 5.7 was also made from polystyrene board, and measured 90.1 cm (L) x 88.0 cm (W) x 4.0 cm (T). Each panel had 80 circular holes an equal distance apart. The panel was flat on one side and had a 1.0 cm deep concave depression on the other side, around each hole, to give the 48.1 (8.3 x 5.8 x 1.0) cubic centimeter of air space used for aeroroot induction.

Nutrient Level Adjuster and Aspirator

Each unit of the DRF hydroponic greenhouse had a nutrient exchange box, which consisted of a nutrient level adjuster and a nutrient outlet plug (Fig. 5.21). Nutrient outlet plugs were set 3.6 m apart in the bottom gutter of the culture bed, connected by a 1" F PVC pipe to the nutrient exchange box. The nutrient level adjuster was made from 5" F ABS plastic tube containing a double set of inner rings (Fig. 5.21). The outer ring was 8 cm high, and two 0.5" F holes were cut at the bottom of the outer ring to allow nutrient solution flowing through and over the inner ring to run back into the reservoir. The inner ring was 3" F in diameter and 8 cm high. This inner ring contained four linked rings, 3, 2, 2 and 1 cm high, respectively. The height of this set of inner rings could be adjusted from 8 cm to 0 cm, according to the state of vegetable growth.

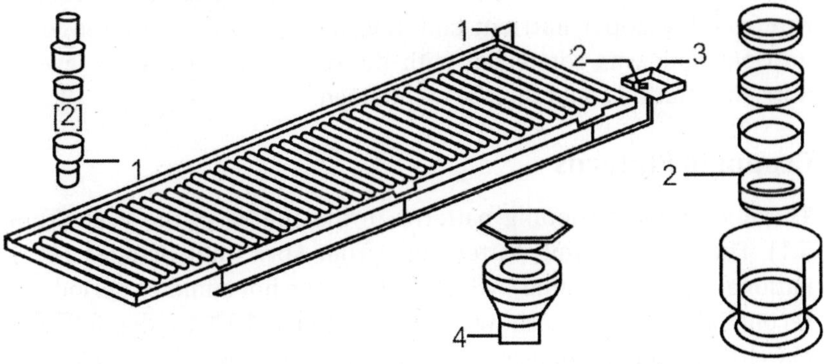

Fig. 5.21: Components of the DRF hydroponic nutrient flow system. 1. Aspirator, 2. Nutrient level adjuster, 3. Nutrient exchange box, 4. Nutrient outlet plug.

In the east side of the culture bed was a 0.5 cm F PVC plastic nutrient supply pipe running into the main gutter. The nutrient supply tube had a tiny hole where it ran through each gully. The aspirator was connected to the nutrient supply pipe at one end, and to the pump at the other end. The aspirator was designed to have a four-bladed propeller inside the tube, while two holes 0.1 cm in diameter were cut opposite each other so that the nutrient solution would absorb more air as it flowed through.

Nutrient Circulation System

The frequency with which the nutrient solution was pumped through the DRF hydroponic system was controlled by an automatic timer insulated within the nutrient controller box. An automatic pumping cycle was set up, with a flow of 6/24 minutes on/off during the daytime, and 6/174 minutes on/off at night. The nutrient in the DRF system was re-circulated. It was first enriched by solution pumped from the reservoir, then passed through the aspirator and the nutrient supply pipe to spray into each gully, collecting in the bottom gutter to run into the nutrient exchange box and back into the reservoir again. A constant concentration of nutrients in the solution was maintained automatically by an insulated floating switch in the lower nutrient tank. When 3% of the total amount of nutrient solution in the DRF hydroponic system had been used, the floating switch automatically turned on to allow twice as much concentrated nutrient solution to run from the upper nutrient tank into the reservoir. Since the lower nutrient tank was connected with the reservoir, a constant level of nutrient solution could thus be maintained.

Cropping Patterns

There were two cropping patterns in the course of the year (Table 5.1). The first cropping pattern was from April until October 10th (a national holiday in China), which covered the hot summer period. The second cropping pattern was from October 10th to the following March. Traditional Chinese leafy vegetables such as pak-choi (*Brassica Chinese* L.), Chinese kale (*Brassica oleracea* L.), leafy mustard (*Brassica juncea* L.), edible amaranth (*Amaranthus tricolor* L.), water convolvulus (*Ipomoea aquatica* Forsk), and leafy lettuce eaten as a cooked vegetable (*Lactuca sativa* L.) etc. were suitable crops for the first cropping pattern. Cucumber (*Cucumis sativus* L.), tomato (*Lycopersicon lycopersicum* L.), muskmelon (*Cucumis melo* L.), celery (*Apium, Graveolens* L.), butterhead or crisp lettuce for salads (*Lactuca sativa* L.), spinach (*Spinacia oleracea* L.), and garland chrysanthemum (*Chrysanthemum coronarium* L.) were selected for the second cropping pattern. Water convolvulus and Chinese leek (*Allium tuberosum* Rottl, ex. K.) were suitable for all-year-round ratoon growth.

Table 5.1: Vegetable cropping patterns in a DRF hydroponic system

<table>
<tr><th rowspan="2">Cropping pattern</th><th colspan="11">Cultivation Calendar</th></tr>
<tr><th>April</th><th>May</th><th>June</th><th>July</th><th>Aug.</th><th>Sept.</th><th>Oct.</th><th>Nov.</th><th>Dec.</th><th>Jan.</th><th>Feb.</th></tr>
<tr><td></td><td colspan="11">Leafy vegetables</td></tr>
<tr><td>I</td><td colspan="6">Pak-choi, Chinese kale, Leafy lettuce, Edible amaranth, Leafy mustard, Water convolvulus, Chinese leek</td><td colspan="5">Garland chrysanthemum, Japanese pak-choi, Celery, Spinach, Salad lettuce, Crisp lettuce, Head lettuce</td></tr>
<tr><td></td><td colspan="6">Leafy vegetables</td><td colspan="5">Fruit vegetables</td></tr>
<tr><td>II</td><td colspan="6">Same as cropping pattern</td><td colspan="5">Tomato, Cucumber, Muskmelon</td></tr>
</table>

Cultural Practices

Vegetable seedlings were grown in a polyfoam (polyurethane sponge) block for several days, the length of time depending on the species of vegetable grown. When the root length of the seedlings reached 3-5 cm or the primary leaf was well developed, the seedlings were transplanted into precut holes in the panels. The root system of the seedlings had to be immersed in the nutrient solution, so that the plants could grow on the ridges of the culture bed. The planting density in each panel varied from 80 to 8 plants, according to the type of vegetable grown. Tall fruit vegetables were supported by a nylon net tied to the overhead frame of the house. Table 5.2 shows the number of days to germination, to the seedling stage, from transplanting to harvest, and planting density, for various vegetable species.

Table 5.2: Days for growth and developmental stage of various vegetable species

Vegetable Species	Growth Stage			Planting Density (plants/panel)
	Germination (days)	Seedling (days)	Harvest (days)	
Pak-choi	1-2	7-10	24	80
Chinese kale	2-3	10-16	30	80
Leaf mustard	1-2	7-14	24	80
Edible amaranth	2-3	10-16	24	80
Water convolvulus	2-3	7-14	24	80

Vegetable Species	Growth Stage			Planting Density (plants/panel)
	Germination (days)	Seedling (days)	Harvest (days)	
Spinach	3-4	10-16	24	80
Garland chrysanthemum	3-4	10-16	24	80
Leafy lettuce	1-3	10-16	24	80
Butterhead lettuce	3-4	16-20	35	8
Crisp lettuce	3-4	16-20	45	8
Celery	7-10	15-20	40	40
Tomato	5-7	20-25	90	9
Cucumber	3-5	15-20	90	4
Muskmelon	3-5	15-20	80	2
Chinese leek	30-40	20-30	20	80

Nutrient Solution

The standard nutrient formula used in the DRF system could be used to grow all kinds of crops, but an increase in microelement concentration was needed for some cropping seasons and vegetable species (Table 5.3 and Table 5.4) **(Kao 1990)**. The concentration of microelements was maintained at a constant level.

Table 5.3: Standard concentration of nutrients in nutrient solutions

Microelement	(me/liter)	Microelement	(ppm)
NO_3-N	6.0	Fe EDTA	2.5
NH_4-N	0.5	B	0.2
PO_4-P	3.0	Mn	0.2
SO_4-S	1.5	Zn	0.01
K	4.0	Cu	0.01
Mg	2.0	Mo	0.01
Ca	4.0		
EC (mmho/cm, 25°C)	1.0		
pH	6.0		

Table 5.4: Nutrient concentration used for growing hydroponic vegetables

Cropping Pattern	Standard concentration (S)	EC (mmho/cm)	pH
I	1.5-2.0 S	1.5-2.0	5.5-6.0
II	2.0-2.5 S	2.0-2.5	6.0-6.5

Adjustment of Nutrients

The nutrient concentration is maintained at a constant level in DRF hydroponics according to the following simulation model (Formula 1).

$$EC_r = \frac{(W - X) \times EC_d}{W} + \frac{X}{W} \times EC_a$$

Formula 1 Simulation model to maintain nutrient concentration at constant level in DFR hydroponics.

- EC_f: Final concentration in hydroponic system (mmho/cm)
- EC_d: Nutrient concentration when measured (mmho/cm)
- EC_a: Additional nutrient concentration (mmho/cm)
- W: Total nutrients in whole hydroponic system (1)
- X: Total nutrients lost from whole hydroponic system (1)

On the basis of this simulation model, nutrient solution stocked in the upper nutrient tank was at a double concentration, and automatically passed through the floating switch to enter the lower nutrient tank, simultaneously running to fill the reservoir up to the set level. The reservoir and the lower tank were designed to connect together, with the floating switch in the lower nutrient tank. Thus, the floating switch began functioning when a 3% loss of the total nutrient solution occurred in the reservoir.

CHAPTER 6

BASIC REQUIREMENTS OF HYDROPONICS

Soils naturally maintain the temperature and aeration needed for root growth. When the soil is poor, plant growth and yield decline due to unsuitable aeration and temperature. Plant cultivation is impossible under ill drained condition. Soil adjusts itself to provide suitable conditions for plant growth. It is called the buffer action of the soils. Plants also absorb nutrients released through natural mineralization.

In a solution or inert medium, maintenance of acidity or alkalinity (pH) and electrical conductivity (EC) in suitable ranges for plant root system is called buffer action. This requirement must be artificially maintained in hydroponics.

In any hydroponics system, the following basic requirements must be maintained at optimum levels:

1. Buffer action of water or the inert medium used.
2. The nutrient solution or the fertilizer mixture used must contain all micro and macro elements necessary for plant growth and development.
3. Buffer action of the nutrient solution must be in the suitable range so that plant root system or the inert medium is not affected.
4. The temperature and aeration of the inert medium or the nutrient solution is suitable for plant root system.

Different requirements for hydroponics has been discussed below:

1. GROWING MEDIA

Growing medium is simply what the roots of the plants are growing in. This can be a vast variety of materials, including Rockwool, perlite, vermiculite, coconut fiber, gravel, sand or any number of other materials, even air can be a growing medium. The growing medium is an inert substance that does not supply any nutrition to the plants, all the nutrition comes from the nutrient solution (water and fertilizer mixed). You can, therefore, easily control everything the plants receive. The strength and pH of the nutrient solution is easy to adjust so that the plants receive just the right amount of nutrient and water. The watering cycles can be simply controlled by an inexpensive timer so that the plants get watered when they need to be.

2. NUTRIENT SOLUTIONS

Mineral nutrition is a broad field, which is concerned with the complex of biosynthetic events by which higher plants produce organic materials from inorganic materials absorbed from their environment. These events include the absorption process itself, the translocation of absorbed mineral nutrients from roots to stems, leaves, fruits and finally conversion of absorbed (inorganic) nutrients to organic form. The nutritional needs of plants were understood when the addition of farmyard manures, plant tissue debris, wood ashes, ground bones, composts, and other materials of plant and animal origin to soils were found to increase their productivity. In the early half of the nineteenth century it was realized that plant growth and development can proceed only when plants are supplied with certain chemical elements referred to as essential elements. These essential elements are mostly derived from mineral constituents of the soil and are absorbed principally by the roots as inorganic ions. Roots are the most important part of the plant as the nutrient uptake takes place mainly through them.

Nutrient solution has been described in other chapter.

3. TEMPERATURE

The plants grow well only when atmospheric temperature is in optimum range. The temperatures that are too high and too low will result in abnormal development and reduced production. The ideal temperature depends on the crops to be selected for growing. Most of the common garden crops, such as tomatoes, cucumbers, lettuce, beans and peas perform well with an average daytime temperature of 78°F and an average night time temperature of 64°F. Winter vegetables, such as cabbage, brussel sprouts, spinach and broccoli should be grown in slightly cooler.

A minimum / maximum thermometer will allow you to track the low and high temperatures in your growing environment. This is important for monitoring overall progress of your hydroponic garden and diagnosing plant growth problems.

For optimum production, heating the root zone is important. For most garden crops 72°F is the ideal root zone temperature. Some growers achieve a heated root area by using heated grow mats placed under the growing medium. Another option is to heat your nutrient solution to the desired temperature and then when your system feeds the plants, the roots are bathed in warm water.

4. FRESH AIR

Plants require adequate air circulation (oxygen) around the plants, as well as proper aeration in the root zone. In soil, adequate oxygen is usually available but plant roots growing in water will quickly exhaust the supply of dissolved oxygen and can be damaged or killed plants unless additional air is provided. Poor ventilation in the growing environment encourages mold, mildew and plant disease. Many hydroponic gardens are located off the floor for better air circulation. Commercial hydroponic greenhouse growers use large fans and air circulation equipment to provide adequate air movement.

5. SHELTER AND SUPPORT

In open field cultivation the soil provide support to the growing plant. But hydroponically grown plants artificial support must be provided usually with string or stakes. In a commercial application, many hydroponic farmers grow their crops inside of a controlled environment greenhouse. This not only provides shelter, but also an ideal, stress-free environment for the plant. Because many hydroponic gardens are quite small and very clean, they can be set up almost anywhere indoors, on a patio or a windowsill, making it easy for the gardener to provide shelter for the plants. In a traditional garden, the soil anchors the plant and provides support. In hydroponics, the growing medium helps support the plant to some extent but most often additional support is needed. Plant stakes, strings, and clips are used for this.

6. WATER

Providing the plants with an adequate amount of water is not difficult in the water culture system, but it can be a problem with the aggregate culture method. If the aggregate is not kept sufficiently moist, the plant roots will dry out and some will die. Even after the proper moisture level being restored, the plants will recover slowly and production will be reduced.

Water quality can be a problem in hydroponic systems. Water with excessive alkalinity or salt content can result in a nutrient imbalance and poor plant growth. Softened water may contain harmful amounts of sodium. Water that tests high in total salts should not be used. Salt levels greater than 0.5 million or 320 parts per million are likely to cause an imbalance of nutrients. The amateur chemist may be able to overcome this problem by custom mixing the nutrient solutions to compensate for the salts in the water.

7. MINERAL NUTRIENTS

Through photosynthesis, green plants manufacture their own organic food, using carbon dioxide and oxygen as raw materials. The nutrients usually supplied to plants by soil are almost entirely mineral salts. Plant physiologists have discovered that plants require carbon, hydrogen, oxygen, nitrogen, phosphorus, potassium, magnesium, sulfur, calcium, iron, manganese, boron, zinc, copper, and probably molybdenum. Carbon, hydrogen, and oxygen are obtained in large quantities from water and air, but the remaining elements are ordinarily supplied as salts by the soil. The relative amount of each of these elements required for normal growth is different in each plant, but all plants require relatively large proportions of nitrogen, phosphorus, potassium, magnesium, sulfur, and calcium. Iron, manganese, boron, zinc, copper, and molybdenum are supplied in minute quantities, and are called micronutrients or trace elements. The specific salts used to supply these elements may be varied at the discretion of the grower; a typical solution of primary minerals is composed of distilled water containing potassium nitrate, KNO_3, calcium nitrate, $Ca(NO_3)_2$, potassium acid phosphate, KH_2PO_4, and magnesium sulfate, $MgSO_4$. In solution, the salts dissociate into ions; potassium nitrate, for example, is available to plants as the ions K^+ and NO_3^-. A solution of micronutrient salts is added to the solution of primary elements to complete the nutrient solution. A small amount of fungicide is usually added in the nutrient solution to prevent the growth of mold.

8. LIGHT

Plants require a constant supply of energy to grow and this energy comes from light. In nature, plants receive light from the sun in a home garden, there is a need to add artificial light so the plants have an adequate amount of light to grow.

There are various types of artificial lights that provide differing light spectrums. Before learning about these artificial lights, it is important to understand how plants use light in the growth process.

Transpiration and photosynthesis are the two major processes that are carried out by green plants using energy from the sun. Both of these processes use large amounts of light energy. Light influences other processes such as flowering, seed germination, certain growth stages and pigment production but, in these cases, only very small amounts of energy from light are used. During the transpiration process, plants draw carbon dioxide from the air through their pores and water from their roots and give off oxygen and water vapor. Energy from the sun evaporates water from the plant cell walls. Although this results in a movement of water in the plant tissue

(xylem). This energy is neither stored nor used to bring about vital reactions involved in the synthesis of foods, in assimilation, growth or reproduction.

In photosynthesis, which literally means "putting together (synthesis) by means of light (photo)," water is drawn up through the stem from the roots and into the leaf tissue where the chloroplasts, containing chlorophyll (a green pigment) can be found. There the water encounters carbon dioxide which entered the leaf from the air through minute breathing pores (stomata) located abundantly on the underside of the leaves. The stomata also permits the outflow of water vapor and oxygen. The light, carbon dioxide and water produce carbohydrates which are stored in the plant and later released as energy for other vital plant functions.

Energy stored as chemical energy in foods (carbohydrates, fats, proteins) is continually released in living cells during the process of respiration. Basically, photosynthesis stores energy and respiration releases it enabling cells to perform the work of living. By releasing energy, respiration provides the energy needed for all other plant functions. All animals ultimately depend on photosynthesis because it is the method by which all basic food is created.

Light is discussed in more details in separate chapter.

CHAPTER 7

GROWING MEDIA

Growing medium is used to lend support to the roots and plants. A variety of growing media and combinations are used for their individual qualities in various types of hydroponic systems. The purpose of growing media is to aerate and support the root system of the plant and to channel the water and nutrients.

The selection of growing medium is largely depend upon availability, the type of hydroponic growing system used and plants to be grown.

The following media are generally found suitable for hydroponics

1. EXPANDED CLAY

This is high performance growing media. The capillary action of this media is very high. Also known as 'hydroton' or 'leca' (= light expanded clay aggregate), trademarked names, these small round baked spheres of clay are inert and are suitable for hydroponic systems in which all the nutrients are carefully controlled in the water. Clay pebbles can be reused provided they are cleaned thoroughly between crops. Baked clay pebbles are highly porous, yet irregularly shaped to create an balance of air space and nutrient solution.

2. ROCKWOOL

Rock wool has become an extremely popular and most widely used growing medium in hydroponics. It is produced from volcanic rock and lime stone. These components are melted at temperature of 2500°C and higher.

The rockwool used in hydroponics consists of mat of long, fine fibre, spun from molten natural rock. Mineral wool, also known as mineral cotton, silicate cotton, stone wool, slag wool, rockwool, and rock wool, is an inorganic substance used for insulation and filtering. It has very high water and air holding capacity and is inorganic, very light when dry, sterile and is not degradable.

Since Rockwool holds 10-14 times as much water as soil and retains 20 percent air, it can be used in any hydroponic system. Although the gardener must be careful of the pH, it can raise the pH of the nutrient solution since Rockwool has a pH of 7.8. Rockwool cannot be used indefinitely and most gardeners only get one use per cube. It is also commonly used for propagation.

It comes in lots of different forms including cubes, blocks, slabs and granulated or flock. When medium is dry, care needs to be taken

so as not inhale any particles. Inhaling such particles may carry a health risk.

It is a poor conductor of heat and sound, is fire-proof and insect-proof, and therefore is ideal as a building insulation. Other uses are in resin bonded panels, growth medium in hydroponics, filler in compounds for gaskets, brake pads, in plastics in the automotive industry and as a filtering medium.

Mineral wool is used for its ability to hold large quantities of water and at the same time maintain a high percentage of air as well. This aids root growth and nutrient uptake. The fibrous nature of mineral wool also provides a good mechanical structure to hold the plant stable. Mineral wool has a high pH, which is unsuitable to plant growth. This requires correcting or conditioning. Conditioned mineral wool has a stable pH over long periods of time.

3. PERLITE

Perlite is a volcanic rock which when heated in excess of 1000°C, expands in to light weight particles. It is used loose or in plastic sleeves immersed in the water. It is also used in potting soil mixes to decrease soil density. Perlite has similar properties and uses to vermiculite but generally holds more air and less water.

In hydroponics, approximately 3 mm particle size should be used. This medium is sterile and is used as a light weight support medium. It does not have high capacity for water retension and has no nutrient holding capacity. Perlite can be used with vermiculite or its own, depending upon specific needs of the plants. Inhelation of the dust must be avoided and this medium is to be prevetted before used.

4. VERMICULITE

Vermiculite is light and have a very high capacity of water retension. It is a natural mineral which expands with the application of heat. It is formed by hydration of certain basaltic minerals, and is often found in association with asbestos.

Expanded vermiculite is used as a soil conditioner, as loose-fill insulating and packing material, as an insulating filler for plaster and concrete compounds, and as a carrier for dry handling and slow release of agricultural chemicals. Vermiculite is often used alongwith perlite as a soil additive for potted plants, and as growing mediums for hydroponics. It requires replacement every 2 to 4 years as its flaky structures breaks down.

Like perlite, vermiculite is another mineral that has been superheated until it has expanded into light pebbles. Vermiculite holds more water than perlite and has a natural "wicking" property that can draw water and nutrients in a passive hydroponic system. If too much water and not enough air surrounds the plants roots, it's possible to gradually lower the medium's water-retention capability by mixing in increasing quantities of perlite.

5. COCO COIR

Coco is a compressed medium created from the husks of coconuts. It is not used generally in hydroponics in India, but due to low cost, it is used in most of the tropical countries. It is not recommended for recirculating systems due to leaching of organics into the water. Coco coir comes also in bags and in slabs. Some types of Coco coir are very high in sodium (salt) due to the nature of Coconut Palms growing on island environments and being processed in the salt air.

6. OASIS ROOT CUBES

An open cell foam cube with a preset pH and a mild fertilizer added, Oasis root cubes produced by Smithers Oasis is the choice of large scale nutrient film growers. It is available in many different sizes. Widely marketed in sheets sized to fit commercial trays (10" x 20"), it is a convenient propagation media. Each sheet is pre-scored for easy removal of a single cube, block of cubes, or strip of cubes. Each cube has been pre-punched with a dibble hole for quick and easy seed or plant cutting insertion.

7. SAND

Coarse washed river sand is a mixture of fine and coarse particles. Sand in the 0.5 mm to 2.5 mm range is most suitable, allowing drainage and good aeration. Between 20-25 per cent by volume of peat moss may be added to improve moisture retention. Builders sand may be used as long as it does not contain large quantities of fine broken shell which will increase the alkalinity of the medium.

8. COARSE FIR SAWDUST

Again, low in cost but not recommended for recirculating systems due to the leaching of large amounts of tannic acid into the water. Canadian tomato growers used this medium to use non-recirculating drip systems with good results. The sawdust must be replaced each season. Orchid growers use fir bark, as it simulates the natural way they grow on trees, and does not hold excess water.

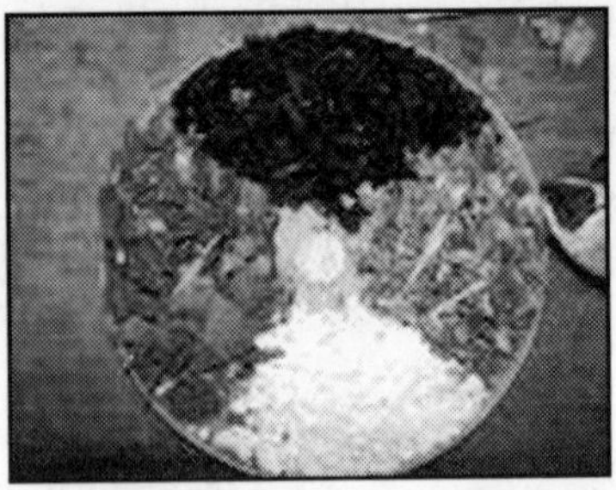

9. CRUSHED GRANITE

In hydroponics, screened crushed granite of approximate particle size of 2 mm should be used. The medium is totally inert, but has a relatively low water retention capacity. The medium can be reused over a period of time.

10. SCORIA

Scoria is a relatively porous volcanic rock which is very good as a medium. Generally a mixture of fine and coarse scoria is used, being heavy enough to support plants yet having good aeration. It is sold as is lava rock in many hardware stores.

CHAPTER 8

EQUIPMENTS AND APPLIANCES

Submersible or ordinary water pumps, EC meter, pH meter are important equipments necessary to operate a circulating hydroponics. PVC pipes can be used as channels in these systems.

1. WATER PUMPS

The water pump must be made up of materials that are non-reactive with nutrient salt solution. Stainless steel shaft, polycarbonate or stainless steel impeller, pump-house and water seal must be there in the pump to be used in hydroponics.

One does not require a pump with very high head for circulating the nutrient solution in hydroponics systems. Therefore, a domestic water pump with 0.5 HP will suffice. A safety device is a must with the water pump as the nutrient solution more effectively conducts electricity compared to water. Therefore, a very sensitive trip switch must be used to disconnect electricity supply whenever the need arises.

2. TIMER AND OXYGEN DETECTION SENSOR

When the plants are small, their oxygen requirement is low. Therefore, the nutrient solution circulating time period can be limited. Limiting the circulating time periods can also reduce the electricity consumption. For this purpose a timer may be used to set the circulating time manually or an oxygen concentration detection sensor may be included in the system, so the sensor can activate the pump whenever the oxygen concentration of the nutrient solution level goes down.

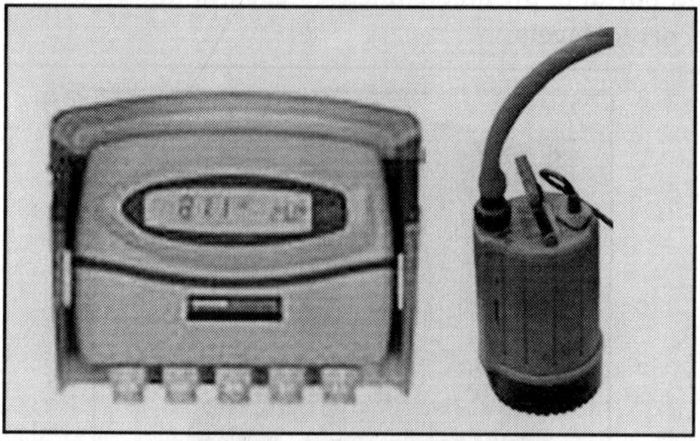

3. PVC PIPES

Type 400 or class 4 100 mm PVC pipes have to be used in circulating hydroponics as the channels. PVC pipes with thinner walls will sag and thereby reduce the flow rate of nutrient solution. The result will be lack of oxygen supply for the plant roots. UV resistant pipelines are preferable. Painting these pipes white will prevent the increase of nutrient solution temperature. The flow rate required in hydroponics is very small ranging from 1 to 3 litres per minute. Therefore, an overflow pipe will have to be fitted to adjust the flow rate.

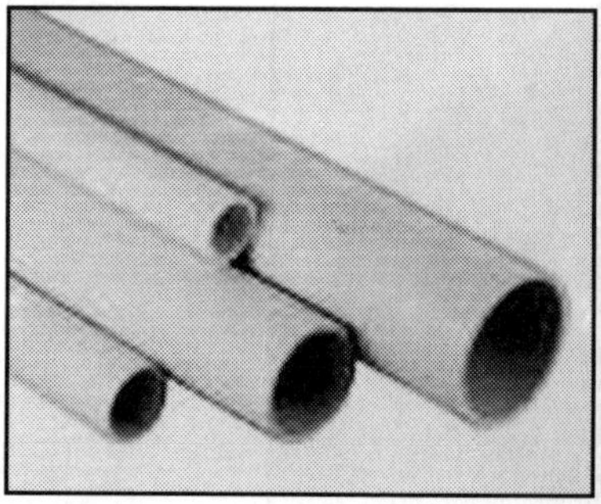

4. pH METER

Simple and portable pH meter must be used to monitor and maintain the pH at correct levels.

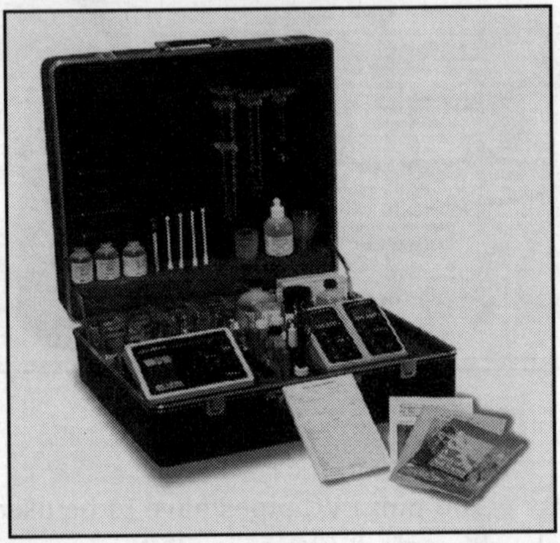

5. BLOWERS

These devices help send airflow through the plants so that plants shake and pollens are distributed to facilitate pollination inside protected structures.

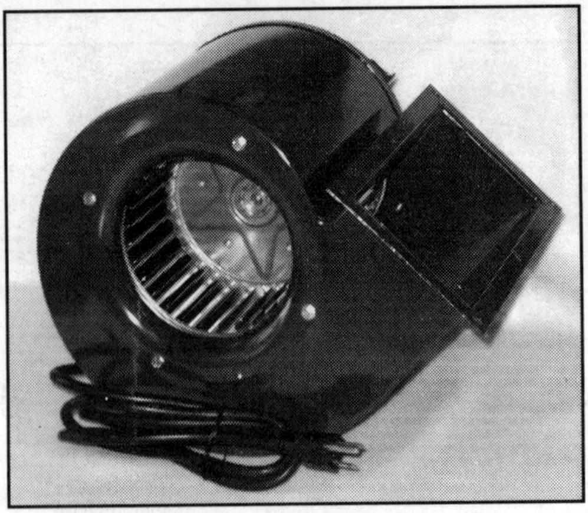

6. POLLINATORS

These simple electrical device vibrate the individual plants when touch them so that pollination is facilitated inside the protected structures.

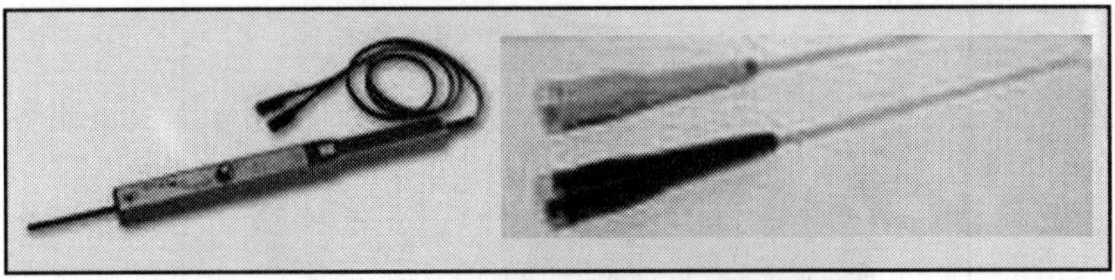

7. NURTIMETER

In addition to the EC, this meter helps measure the nutrient contents of the solution.

8. EC METER

Electrical conductivity is a measure of the rate at which a small electric current flows through a solution. Electrical conductivity (EC) of the nutrient solution can be measured by EC Meter. It usually shows the reading in either mmhos per centimeter (uMhos/cm) or microsiemens per centimeter (uS/cm). 1 uMhos/cm is equivalent to 1 uS/cm.

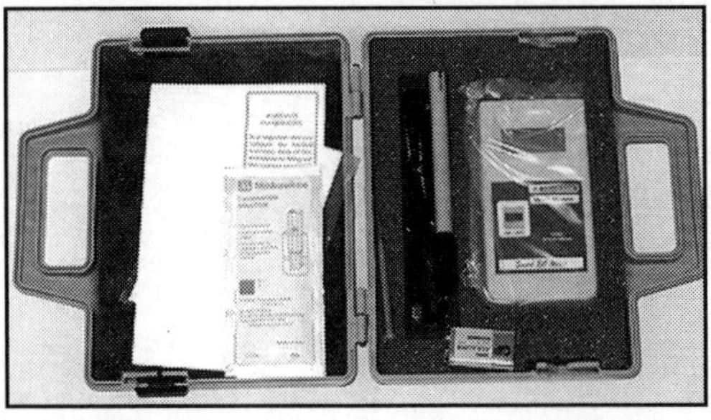

9. TDS METER

The determination of total dissolved solids (TDS) of nutrient solution is necessary to know the strength of solution. It can be measured by

TDS Meter which usually shows the reading in milligarm per litre (mg/l) or parts per million (ppm). Water Pump Spray pump

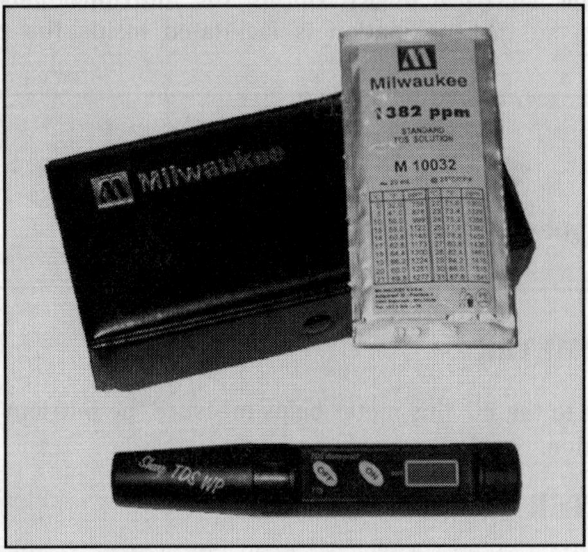

CHAPTER 9

NUTRIENT SOLUTIONS FOR HYDROPONICS

ESSENTIAL PLANTS NUTRIENTS

Plants require 17 essential elements for their growth and development. Without these nutrients plants cannot complete their life cycles and their roles in plant growth cannot be replaced by any other elements.

All essential elements are classified as under:

1. **Macro nutrients**: Which required by the plants in large quantity i.e. more than 1 ppm.
   a) Carbon (C), Hydrogen (H), Oxygen (O)
   b) C, H, O are called structural elements
   c) Nitrogen (N), Phosphorus (P), Potassium (K)
   d) N, P, K are called primary elements
   e) Calcium (Ca), Magnesium (Mg), Sulphur (S)
   f) Ca, Mg, S are called secondary elements
2. **Micro nutrients:** Which required by the plants in small quantity i.e. less than 1 ppm. These nutrients are also trace elements.
   a) iron (Fe), chlorine (Cl), boron (B), manganese (Mn), copper (Cu), zinc (Zn), molybdenum (Mo) and nickel (Ni).

CRITERIA USED FOR CONSIDERING ELEMENTS AS ESSENTIAL

The criteria as to which element should be considered as essential was given by Arnon as follows:

1. The plant is unable to grow normally and complete its life cycle, in the absence of the elements.
2. The element is specific and cannot be replaced by another element however close it may be in the periodic table.
3. The element plays a direct role in the metabolism of the plant.

INDIVIDUAL PLANT NUTRIENTS OF HYDROPONIC SOLUTION

Careful experiments using hydroponics have shown that each of the nutrients needed by the plant has a very specific function in plant growth as explained below:

Nitrogen

Nitrogen is a component of proteins, which form an essential part of protoplasm and also occur as stored foods in plant cells. Nitrogen is also a part of other organic compounds in plants such as chlorophyll, amino acids, alkaloids and some plant hormones.

Sulphur

Sulphur forms a part of the protein molecule. Plant proteins may have from 0.5- 1.5% of this element. The sulphydryl group is a very important group essential for the action of certain enzymes and co-enzymes. In additional, sulphur is a constituent of ferredoxin and of some lipids.

Phosphorous

This element is also a component of some plant proteins, phospholipids, sugar phosphates, nucleic acids, ATP and NADP. The highest percentages of phosphorous occur in the parts of the plant that are growing rapidly.

Potassium

Potassium accumulates in tissues that are growing rapidly. It will migrate from older tissues to meristematic regions. For example, during the maturing of the crop there is movement of potassium from leaves into the fruit.

Calcium

All ordinary green plants require calcium. It is one of the constituents of the middle lamella of the cell wall, where it occurs in the form of calcium pectate. Calcium affects the permeability of cytoplasmic membranes and the hydration of colloids. Calcium may be found in combination with organic acids in the plant.

Magnesium

Magnesium is a constituent of chlorophyll. It occupies a central position in the molecule. Chlorophylls are the only major compounds of plants that contain magnesium as a stable component. Many enzyme reactions, particularly those involving a transfer of phosphate, are activated by magnesium ions.

Iron

A number of essential compounds in plants contain iron in a form that is bound firmly into the molecule. Iron plays a role in being the site on some electron carriers where electrons are absorbed and then given off during electron transport. The iron atom is alternately reduced and then oxidized. Iron plays a very important role in energy conversion reactions of both photo synthesis and transpiration.

Boron

Although the exact function of boron in plant metabolism is unclear, boron does plays regular role in carbohydrate breakdown. Symptoms of boron deficiency include stunted roots and shoot elongation, lack of flowering, darkening of tissues and growth abnormalities.

Zinc

Zinc is essential to the normal development of a variety of plants. Large quantities of zinc are toxic to plants.

Manganese

The importance of manganese as an activator of several enzymes of aerobic respiration explains some of the disruptive effects of a manganese deficiency on metabolism. The most obvious sign of a manganese deficiency is chlorosis. Manganese chlorosis results in the leaf taking on a mottled appearance.

Copper

Copper is a constituent of certain enzyme systems, such as ascorbic acid oxidize and cytochrome oxidize. In addition, copper is found in plastocyanin, part of the electron-transport chain in photosynthesis.

Molybdenum

Molybdenum is important in enzyme systems involved in nitrogen fixation and nitrate reduction. Plants suffering molybdenum deficiency can absorb nitrate ions but are unable to use this form of nitrogen.

FUNCTION OF MINERALS

The important functions of minerals are as follows:

1. Protoplasmic Elements

Nitrogen, Phosphorus and Sulphur are considered as protoplasmic elements as they form part of protoplasm along with carbon, hydrogen and oxygen.

2. Balancing Elements

Calcium, Magnesium and Potassium counteract the toxic effect of other minerals by causing ionic balance.

3. Framework Elements

Carbon, Hydrogen and Oxygen are considered as framework elements because they constitute the carbohydrates, which form cell walls.

4. Influence on the Osmotic Pressure of the Cells

Plant cells contain dissolved mineral elements in the cell sap, which influences the osmotic pressure of the cell.

5. Catalytic Elements

Some elements function as part of the enzyme i.e., without the presence of these elements some enzyme cannot function.

Plant nutrients are dissolved in the water used in hydroponics and are mostly in inorganic and ionic form. Primary among the dissolved cations (positively-charged ions) are Ca^{2+} (calcium), Mg^{2+} (magnesium), and K^{+} (potassium); the major nutrient anions in nutrient solutions are NO_3^- (nitrate), SO_4^{2-} (sulfate), and $H_2PO_4^-$ (phosphate).

Numerous 'recipes' for hydroponic solutions are available. Many use different combinations of chemicals to reach similar total final compositions. Commonly-used chemicals for the macronutrients include potassium nitrate, calcium nitrate, potassium phosphate, and magnesium sulfate.

NUTRIENT SOLUTION

All essential nutrients are supplied to hydroponics plants in the form of nutrient solution, which consists of fertilizers salts dissolved in water. The hydroponic grower must have a good knowledge of the plant nutrients, as management of plant nutrition through management of nutrient solution is the key to success in hydroponic gardening. The hydroponic methods enable growers to control the availability of essential elements by adjusting or changing the nutrient solution to suit the plant growth stage and to provide them in balanced amounts. As the nutrients are present in ionic forms in the nutrient solution and also, not needing to search or compete for available nutrients as they do in soil, hydroponic plants reach maturity much sooner. Optimization of plant nutrition is easily achieved in hydroponics than in soil.

Various micronutrients are typically added to hydroponic solutions to supply essential elements; among them are Fe (iron), Mn (manganese), Cu (copper), Zn (zinc), B (boron), Cl (chlorine), and Ni (nickel). Chelating agents are sometimes used to keep Fe soluble. These nutrients are essential elements that plants need in very small amounts. Without these trace elements plants can become sick and develop all sorts of problems, depending on which micro-nutrient(s) are missing. In the case of food crops, the lack of micro-nutrients in the soil can mean a lack of nutrients in the food, which means at best that the food isn't as healthy as it could be and at worst that people can develop heath problems due to the lack of these essential elements. Always use quality hydroponic fertilizer.

Plants will change the composition of the nutrient solutions upon contact by depleting specific nutrients more rapidly than others, removing water from the solution, and altering the pH by excretion of either acidity or alkalinity. Care is required not to allow salt concentrations to become too high, nutrients to become too depleted, or pH to wander far from the desired value.

Chelating Agents

The micronutrient cations iron, and to a lesser extent zinc, manganese, and copper, are relatively insoluble in nutrient solutions when provided as common inorganic salts, and they are also rather insoluble in most soils. This insolubility is especially marked if the pH is above 5, as it is in nearly all soils with low rainfall. Under these conditions, micronutrient cations react with hydroxyl ions, eventually precipitating insoluble hydrous metal oxides. An example in which the ferric form of iron yields the reddish-brown oxide (rust) is shown in the reaction below-

$$2Fe^{3+} + 6OH^- \rightarrow 2Fe(OH)_3 \rightarrow Fe_2O_3.3H_2O$$

Due to insolubility, these micronutrients must be held in solution by some other agents, which are known as ligand or chelating agent or chelator. Reaction of a divalent or trivalent metal ion with a ligand forms a chelate (from the Greek, *claw like*). *A chelate is the soluble product formed when certain atoms in an organic ligand donate electrons to the cation.* Negatively charged carboxyl groups and nitrogen atoms possess electrons that can be shared in this way. In calcareous soils (those rich in Ca^{2+} and with a pH generally of 7 or higher), more than 90 percent of the copper and manganese and half or more of the zinc are probably chelated with microbiologically produced organic compounds.

PREPARATION OF NUTRIENT SOLUTION

Hydroponic growers can formulate their own fertilizer mixtures to prepare nutrient solutions using completely water soluble nutrients salts. A number of formulations are available in the market to choose.

Table 9.1: The average concentration of plant nutrient in plant solution (in ppm = parts per million)

S.No.	Nutrients	Cocnetration (PPM)
1.	Nitrogen (nitrate form)	70 –300
2.	Nitrogen (ammonium form)	0 –31
3.	Potassium	200 –400
4.	Phosphorous	30 –90
5.	Calcium	150 –400
6.	Sulfur	60 –330
7.	Magnesium	25 –75
8.	Iron	5 -5.0
9.	Boron	1 -1.0
10.	Manganese	1 -1.0
11.	Zinc	02 -.2
12.	Molybdenum	01 -.1
13.	Copper	02 -.2

Table 9.2: Compatibility chart for different fertilizers for hydroponics

Soluble fertilizers	AN	AS	CAN	MAP	SOP	MOP
Ammonium nitrate	-	C	C	C	C	C
Ammonium sulphate	C	-	L	C	C	C
Calcium ammonium nitrate	C	L	-	X	C	C
Mono ammonium phosphate	C	C	X	-	C	C
Potassium sulphate	C	C	L	C	-	C
Potassium chloride	C	C	X	C	C	-
Gypsum	X	X	X	X	C	C
Potassium nitrae	C	L	C	C	-	C

C = Compatible (Can be mixed in solution), L = limited compatibility (mix at the time of use or some precautions must be taken), X = Incompatible (cannot be mixed).

It is important to avoid any formulations that contain impurities like sand, clay or silt. Such impurities do not supply any nutrients but they are harmful as they can block the delivery tubes. Also avoid any formulation that has insoluble or less soluble salts. In hydroponics, the nutrients must be available in solution in ionic form for plant absorption. If they are found as salts, plants will suffer from nutrient deficiency symptoms. Although urea is completely soluble in water, it cannot be used in hydroponics, as it does not break into ionic form in the solution. Some fertilizer salts react with each other to produce insoluble precipitations.

For example, ammonium sulphate and potassium chloride form less soluble potassium sulphate in the tank. Phosphate fertilizers act problematic in the presence of high calcium and magnesium concentrations, causing precipitation of low soluble phosphates. Therefore, select fertilizers that are compatible with each other. The Table 9.2 indicates compatibility of some salts fertilizer mixtures for hydroponics.

NUTRIENT SOLUTION MANAGEMENT

While optimum nutrition is easy to achieve in hydroponics, incorrect management of the nutrient solution can damage the plants and lead to complete failure. The success or failure of a hydroponic garden therefore, depends primarily on the strict nutrient management programme. Carefully manipulating the nutrient solution pH level, temperature and electrical conductivity and replacing the solution whenever necessary, will lead to a successful hydroponic garden.

pH LEVEL

Perhaps one of the most overlooked aspects of gardening, pH is very important in hydroponic and organic as well as regular "dirt" gardening. pH is measured on a scale of 1 to 14 with 7 being "neutral". Acids are lower than 7 and alkalis (bases) are above 7.

To be technical, the term pH refers to the potential hydrogen-hydroxyl ion content of a solution. Solutions ionize into positive and negative ions. If the solution has more hydrogen (positive) ions, than hydroxyl (negative) ions then it is an acid (1-6.9 on the pH scale). Conversely, if the solution has more hydroxyl ions than hydrogen it is alkaline (or base), with a range of 7.1 to 14 on the pH scale.

Pure water has a balance of hydrogen (H+) and hydroxyl (OH-) ions and is therefore pH neutral (pH 7). When the water is less than pure, it can have a pH either higher or lower than 7.

The pH scale is logarithmic, which means that each unit of change equals a ten fold change in the hydrogen / hydroxyl ion concentration. To put it another way, a solution with a pH of 6.0 is 10 times more acidic than a solution with a value of pH 7.0, and a solution with a pH value of 5.0 would be 10 times more acidic than the solution of 6.0 pH and 100 times more acidic than the solution with a 7.0 pH. This means that when you are adjusting the pH of your nutrient solution and you need to move it 2 points (example: 7.5 to 5.5) you would have to use 10 times more adjuster than if you were moving the pH value just 1 point (7.5 to 6.5).

In simple terms, pH is a measure of acidity or alkalinity on a scale of 1 to 14. In a nutrient solution, pH determines the availability of essential plant elements. A solution is considered to be neutral at pH 7.0, alkaline if above and acidic if below. For pH values above 7.5, iron, manganese, copper, zinc and boron becomes less available to plants.

Should the pH of a nutrient solution fall below 6.0, then the solubility of phosphoric acid, calcium and manganese drops sharply. The optimum pH range for hydroponic nutrient solution is between 5.8 and 6.5. Nutrient deficiencies will become apparent or toxicity symptoms will develop if the pH is higher or lower than the recommended range for individual crops. For example, if pH is consistently 7.5, one can expect intraveinal chlorosis to occur, an indication of iron deficiency.

The control of pH in nutrient solution is extremely important, not just with hydroponics but in soil as well. Plants lose the ability to absorb different nutrients when the pH is not at the proper level. Most plants can grow hydroponically within a pH range of 5.8 to 6.8, 6.3 is considered optimal. The pH in a hydroponic system is much easier to check than the pH of soil. Many hardware, pet, and hydroponic supply stores sell pH-testing kits. Testing pH is easy and essential in a hydroponics system. If the pH is too high or too low, the plant will not be able to absorb certain nutrients and will show signs of deficiencies. pH should be checked once a week. It is easy to adjust by adding small amounts of soluble Potash to raise pH, or phosphoric acid to lower pH. The ability to quickly and easily test and control pH in hydroponics is a major advantage over dirt gardening, where testing and adjusting the pH is much more complicated and time consuming.

When plants absorb nutrients and water from solution, pH of the solution changes. Therefore, it must be monitored daily, and adjusted to be between the recommended ranges. Chemical buffers can adjust the pH of a nutrient solution, when it strays outside the ideal. It can be lowered by adding dilute concentrations of phosphoric or nitric acids and raised by adding a dilute concentration of potassium hydroxide. Although it is important to stay within recommended range, it is far more important to prevent large fluctuations.

WHY IS pH IMPORTANT?

When the pH is not at the proper level, the plant will lose its ability to absorb some of the essential elements required for healthy growth. For all plants, there is a particular pH level that will produce optimum results (Table 9.3). This pH level will vary from plant to plant, but in general most plants prefer a slightly acid growing environment (between 6.0 - 6.5), although most plants can still survive in an environment with a pH of between 5.0 and 7.5.

Table 9.3: pH Values for different Hydroponic Crops

S.No.	Plant	pH Range
1.	Beans	6.0-6.5
2.	Broccoli	6.0-6.5
3.	Cabbage	6.5-7.5
4.	Cantaloupe	6.5-6.8
5.	Carrots	5.8-6.4
6.	Chives	6.0-6.5
7.	Cucumbers	5.8-6.0
8.	Egg plants	5.7 – 5.9
9.	Garlic	6.0-6.5
10.	Lettuce	6.0-6.5
11.	Melons	5.4-5.6
12.	Onions	6.5-7.0
13.	Peas	6.0-6.8
14.	Peppers	5.8-6.2
15.	Pineapple	5.0-5.5
16.	Pumpkin	5.0-6.5
17.	Radish	6.0-7.0
18.	Strawberries	5.5-6.5
19.	Tomatoes	5.5-6.5

When pH rises above 6.5, some of the nutrients and micro-nutrients begin to precipitate out of solution and can stick to the walls of the reservoir and growing chambers. For example: Iron will be about half precipitated at the pH level of 7.3 and at about 8.0 there is virtually no iron left in solution at all. In order for your plants to use the nutrients they must be dissolved in the solution. Once the nutrients have precipitated out of solution the plants can no longer absorb them and will suffer (or die). Some nutrients will precipitate out of solution when the pH drops also.

CHECKING OF pH

When you are growing plants hydroponically, checking and adjusting pH is a simple matter, it can be a bit more complicated when growing organically or in dirt. There are several ways to check the pH of the nutrient solution in your hydroponic system.

Paper test strips are probably the most inexpensive way to check the pH of the nutrient solution. These paper strips are impregnated with a pH sensitive dye which changes color when dipped into the nutrient solution. The paper strip is then compared to a color chart to determine the pH level of the solution being checked. These test strips are inexpensive, but sometimes they can be hard to read, because the colors differences can be subtle.

Liquid pH test kits are probably the most popular method to check pH for the hobby gardeners. These liquid test kits work by adding a few drops of a pH sensitive dye to a small amount of the nutrient solution and then comparing the color of the resulting liquid with a color chart. The liquid kits are a bit more expensive than the paper test strips but they work very well, and are normally easier to "read" than the paper indicator strips.

The Most high-tech way to check pH is to use the digital meters. These meters come in a huge array of sizes and prices. The most popular type of pH meter for the hobby gardeners are the digital "pens". These pens are manufactured by several different companies and are very handy and easy to use. You simply dip the electrode into the nutrient solution for a few moments and the pH value is displayed on a LCD display.

The pH meters are very accurate (when properly calibrated) and fast. They need to cared for properly, otherwise, they will quit working. The glass bulb electrode must be kept clean and wet at all times. The pH meters are actually very sensitive and are susceptible to problems with the electrode.

The pH meters are slightly temperature sensitive. Many of the pH meters on the market have Automatic Temperature Compensation (ATC), which corrects the reading with respect to temperature. On meters without ATC, the pH should be checked at the same time of day each time in order to minimize any temperature related fluctuations.

The pH meters usually need to be calibrated frequently, as the meters can "drift" and to insure accuracy you must check calibration often. The tip needs to be stored in a electrode storage solution or in a buffer solution. The tip should never be allowed to dry out.

Due to the fact that pH meters have a reputation of breaking down without warning, it is a good idea to keep an emergency back up for checking pH (paper test strips or a liquid pH test kit), just in case.

Adjusting pH

There are several chemicals used by the hobby gardeners to adjust pH. The most popular are probably phosphoric acid (to lower pH), and potassium hydroxide (to raise pH). Both of these chemicals are relatively safe, although they can cause burns and should never come in contact with the eyes. Most hydroponic supply stores sell pH adjusters that are diluted to a level that is reasonably safe and easy to use. Concentrated adjusters can cause large pH changes and can make adjusting the pH very frustrating.

Several other chemicals can be used to adjust the pH of hydroponic nutrient solutions. Nitric acid and sulfuric acid can be used to lower pH but are much more dangerous than phosphoric acid. Food grade citric acid is sometimes used in organic gardening to lower pH.

Always add the nutrients to the water before checking and adjusting the pH of your nutrient solution. The fertilizer will usually lower the pH of the water due to its chemical make up. After adding nutrient and mixing the solution, check the pH using what ever means you have. If the pH needs to be adjusted, add the appropriate adjuster. Use small amounts of pH adjuster until you get familiar with the process. Recheck the pH and repeat the above steps until the pH level is where you want it to be.

The pH of the nutrient solution will have a tendency to go up as the plants use the nutrients. As a result the pH needs to be checked periodically (and adjusted if necessary). To start out I suggest that you check pH on a daily basis. Each system will change pH at a different rate depending on a variety of factors. The type of growing medium used, the weather, kind of plants and even the age of the plants all effect the pH variations.

ELECTRICAL CONDUCTIVITY (EC)

The electrical conductivity indicates the strength of nutrient solution, as measured by an EC meter. The unit for measuring EC is dSm^{-1}. A limitation of EC is that it indicates only the total concentration of the solution and not the individual nutrient components. The ideal EC range for hydroponics is between 1.5 and 2.5 dS/m. Higher EC will prevent nutrient absorption due to osmotic pressure and lower EC severely affect plant health and yield. When plants take up nutrients and water from the solution, the total salt concentration, i.e., the EC of the solution changes. If the EC is higher than the recommended range, fresh water must be added to reduce it. If it is lower, add nutrients to raise it.

Measuring Conductivity

Conductivity is a measure of the rate at which a small electric current flows through a solution. When the concentration of nutrients is greater, the current will flow faster. When the concentration of the nutrients is lower, the current will flow slower.

You can measure your nutrient solution to determine how strong or weak it is with an EC (electrical conductivity) or TDS (total dissolved solids) meter. An EC meter usually shows the reading in either micro mhs per centimeter (μMho/cm) or microsiemens per centimeter (μS/cm). 1.0 μMho/cm is equivalent to 1.0 uS/cm. A TDS meter usually shows the reading in milligrams per liter (mg/l) or parts per million (ppm).

EC is generally measured at 25°C. If the temperature of the solution is raised, the EC will read higher, even though no nutrients have been added. If the temperature drops below 25°C, the EC will decrease.

Table 9.4: Some general guidelines for EC levels

Growth stage/Condition	**Fruiting Plants (such as tomatoes, cucumbers)**	**Leafy Plants (such as lettuce, basil)**
Initial Growth (seedling stage)	1600 -1800 mMho/cm 1120 -1260 ppm	1400 -1600 mMho /cm 980 -1120 ppm
Average EC	2500 mMho/cm 1750 ppm	1800 mMho/cm 1260 ppm
Fruiting	2400 -2600 mMho/cm 1680 -1820 ppm	-
Low light conditions (winter)	2800 -3000 mMho/cm 2000 ppm	2000 mMho/cm 1320 ppm
High light conditions (summer)	2200 -2400 mMho/cm 1700 ppm	1600 mMho/cm 1120 ppm

Therefore, it is important to always measure your EC at a consistent temperature of 25°C. Some EC and TDS meters compensate for varying temperatures.

Another measurement in conductivity is CF (conductivity factor) which is expressed on a scale of 1 to 100. Pure water containing no nutrients is rated at 0 and maximum strength nutrients would rate 100.

In low light conditions (winter), a hydroponic grower should increase the concentration of nutrients in solution in a hydroponic garden. In high light conditions (summer), a hydroponic grower should decrease the concentration of nutrients in solution in a hydroponic garden.

CONCENTRATION OF DISSOLVED OXYGEN (DO)

The concentration of dissolved oxygen (DO) in the nutrient solution decreases with an increase in the ambient temperature (**Douglas 1976, Resh 1987**). This results in an undesirable fall in the respiration rate of the hydroponic roots, due to the shortage of DO in high-temperature nutrient solution (**Kao 1988**). The dissolved oxygen level could be forced upwards by prolonging the nutrient circulation period — i.e. by a non-stop flow in NFT — but the amount of electricity consumed meant that this was of little practical use. The aspirator was a special device used in the DRF hydroponic system to increase the DO in the nutrient solution automatically while the circulation system was operating. The aspirators could oxygenate nutrient solution being pumped at 7.5-8.0 liters / minute, so that the solution was saturated with DO (**Kao 1987**). Nineteen or twenty aspirators could be operated simultaneously by a 1 HP pump.

The nutrient level adjuster placed in the nutrient exchange box of the DRF hydroponic system was used to increase DO by producing an alternation of 1-2 cm in the depth of the nutrient solution. The height of the outer ring of the nutrient level adjuster was fixed at 8 cm, while that of the inner ring could be adjusted. It was found in DFT that the depth of the nutrient solution fell rapidly to its original level 10 minutes after pumping stopped, while this was delayed to 24 minutes in DRF. Thus, the function of the nutrient level adjuster was to move the level of nutrient solution up and down in the culture bed. In NFT, since the flow of the nutrient solution was continuous, DO could be kept at 45-50% of saturation level. However, if the room temperature reached 37°C, the DO in NFT fell to 30-40% of saturation level, reducing the growth vigor of vegetable crops.

AUTOMATIC MANAGEMENT OF NUTRIENT SOLUTION

Routine management of the nutrient solution in the DRF hydroponic system was controlled according to a simulation model, as mentioned above. We found that if $X/W < 3\%$ and $EC_d/EC_a < 1\%$, then EC_f would tend to become equal to EC_a after additional nutrient solution had been supplied for 24 days (**Kao 1990**). It is observed that nutrient solution concentration in hydroponically grown pak-choi was not significantly different to the simulated curve during 24 days of operation. If the nutrient concentration is not adjusted, the nutrient status varies, resulting in lower yield potential. Table 9.4 shows variations in the nutrient status and fresh weight of pak-choi during a 24-day growing period, during which the pH in the treatment in which conditions were controlled was raised to 7.8 and the EC was reduced to 1.1 mmho/cm if the plants were grown at 17-21°C. At 27-31°C, the pH was kept at 4.9 and the EC at 2.9 mmho/cm. If the pH and EC were not controlled, there was a fresh weight loss of 34-36%.

pH

The formula for calculating pH is:

$$pH = -\log_{10} [H^+]$$

$[H^+]$ indicates the activity of H^+ ions (also written $[H_3O^+]$, the equivalent hydronium ions), measured in moles per litre (also known as molarity). In dilute solutions (like river or tap water) the activity is approximately equal to the concentration of the H^+ ion.

In aqueous solution at standard temperature and pressure, a pH of 7 indicates neutrality (i.e. pure water) because water naturally dissociates into H^+ and OH^- ions with equal concentrations of 1×10^{-7} M. A lower pH number (for example pH 3) indicates increasing strength of acidity, and a higher pH number (for example pH 11) indicates increasing strength of alkalinity.

Most substances have a pH in the range 0 to 14, although extremely acidic or basic substances may have $pH < 0$, or $pH > 14$.

In nonaqueous solutions or non-STP conditions, the pH of neutrality may not be 7. Instead it is related to the dissociation constant for the specific solvent used.

Measuring

pH can be measured by addition of a pH indicator into the studying solution. The indicator color varies depending on the pH of the solution. Using indicators, qualitative determinations can be made with universal indicators that have broad color variability over a wide pH range and quantitative determinations can be made using indicators that have strong color variability over a small pH range. Extremely precise measurements can be made over a wide pH range using indicators that have multiple equilibriums (i.e. H_2I) in conjunction with spectrophotometric methods to determine each of components that make up the color of solution by using a pH meter together with pH-selective electrodes (pH glass electrode, hydrogen electrode, quinhydrone electrode and other).

Table 9.5: Some common pH values

Substance	pH	Substance	pH
Battery acid	<1.0	Human Saliva in Cancer patients	4.5-5.7
Gastric acid	2.0	Milk	6.5
Lemon juice	2.4	Pure water	7.0
Cola	2.5	Human Saliva	6.5-7.4
Vinegar	2.9	Blood	7.34 - 7.45
Orange or apple juice	3.5	Sea water	8.0
Beer	4.5	Hand soap	9.0 - 10.0
Coffee	5.0	Household ammonia	11.5
Tea	5.5	Bleach	12.5
Acid rain	< 5.6	Household lye	13.5

pOH

There is also pOH, in a sense the opposite of pH, which measures the concentration of OH^- ions. Since water self ionizes, and notating $[OH^-]$ as the concentration of hydroxide ions, we have

$$K_w = [H^+][OH^-]=10^{-14} \ (*)$$

where K_w is the ionization constant of water.

Now, since

$$\log K_w = \log [H^+] + \log [OH^-]$$

by logarithmic identities, we then have the relationship

$$-14 = \log [H^+] + \log [OH^-] \ (*)$$

and thus

$$pOH = -\log [OH^-] = 14 + \log [H^+] = 14 - pH \ (*)$$

(*) Valid for temperature = 298 K (24.85°C) only.

Calculation of pH for Weak and Strong Acids

Values of pH for weak and strong acids can be approximated using certain assumptions.

Under the Brønsted-Lowry theory, stronger or weaker acids are a relative concept. But here we define a strong acid as a species which is a much stronger acid than the hydronium (H_3O^+) ion. In that case the dissociation reaction (strictly $HX + H_2O \leftrightarrow H_3O^+ + X^-$ but simplified as $HX \leftrightarrow H^+ + X^-$) goes to completion, i.e. no unreacted acid remains in solution. Dissolving the strong acid HCl in water can therefore be expressed:

$$HCl(aq) \rightarrow H^+ + Cl^-$$

This means that in a 0.01 M solution of HCl it is approximated that there is a concentration of 0.01 M dissolved hydrogen ions. From above, the pH is: $pH = -\log_{10} [H^+]$:

$$pH = -\log(0.01)$$

which equals 2.

For weak acids, the dissociation reaction does not go to completion. An equilibrium is reached between the hydrogen ions and the conjugate base. The following shows the equilibrium reaction between methanoic acid and its ions:

$$HCOOH(aq) \leftrightarrow H^+ + HCOO^-$$

It is necessary to know the value of the equilibrium constant of the reaction for each acid in order to calculate its pH. In the context of pH, this is termed the *acidity constant* of the acid but is worked out in the same way (see chemical equilibrium):

$$K_a = [\text{hydrogen ions}][\text{acid ions}] / [\text{acid}]$$

For HCOOH, $K_a = 1.6 \times 10^{-4}$.

When calculating the pH of a weak acid, it is usually assumed that the water does not provide any hydrogen ions. This simplifies the calculation, and the concentration provided by water, 1×10^{-7} mol, is usually insignificant.

With a 0.1 mol solution of methanoic acid (HCOOH), the acidity constant is equal to:

$$K_a = [H^+][HCOO^-] / [HCOOH]$$

Given that an unknown amount of the acid has dissociated, [HCOOH] will be reduced by this amount, while [H^+] and [$HCOO^-$] will each be increased by this amount. Therefore, [HCOOH] may be replaced by 0.1 –&; x, and [H^+] and [$HCOO^-$] may each be replaced by x, giving us the following equation:

$$1.6 \times 10^{-4} = \frac{x^2}{0.1 - x}$$

Solving this for *x* yields 3.9×10^{-3}, which is the concentration of hydrogen ions after dissociation. Therefore the pH is $-\log(3.9\times10^{-3})$, or about 2.4.

Neutralization

Neutralization can be summed up by the equation:

$$H^+ + OH^- \Rightarrow H_2O$$
(acid + base ⇒ water)

A simple, common example with HCl and NaOH yielding salt water:

$$HCl + NaOH \Rightarrow H^+ + Cl^- + Na^+ + OH^- \Rightarrow H_2O + NaCl$$

DRIP (SUBSTRATE)

The drip system is often used in commercial hydroponic facilities that grow long term crops like tomatoes, cucumbers and peppers. In this system, the nutrient solution is delivered to the plants through drip emitters on a timed system. The emitters are usually scheduled to run for approximately 10 minutes of every hour depending on the stage of development of the plant and the amount of available light. The drip cycle flushes the growing medium, providing the plants with fresh nutrients, water and oxygen.

In a commercial drip system, the plant roots are most commonly grown in a medium of perlite or rockwool. The biggest variables in a drip system are in the growing medium and the container that holds that medium. Perlite is often bagged in thin, plastic sleeves. Holes are cut in the bag and plants, usually 3-4, are set in with the roots growing down into the perlite. Recently, a bucket system has been developed to contain perlite for drip systems. Each bucket holds loose perlite and one or two plants. In either of these methods, a slot or hole is cut in the container to allow excess nutrient solution to run out. A drain line below the bag or bucket collects the excess.

Another method of a drip system that is becoming popular for lettuce and herb production is the perlite tray, usually about 24 inches wide by 10-14 feet long. An aluminum tray, coated with a non-toxic material, is filled with perlite and set on a gentle slope of 1-inch to 10-feet. The nutrient solution is continuously dripped in at the higher end of the tray and allow to trickle through the perlite to the other end. Essentially, this system is a combination of drip and NFT techniques.

In most drip systems, injectors are used to add nutrient concentrates to water when the feed cycle starts. In this case, there is no need for a large nutrient reservoir tank or the periodic dumping of used nutrient.

FERTILIZER MIXTURES FOR HYDROPONICS

A gardener can purchase all essential minerals separately and mix to prepare their own hydroponic fertilizer. Unfortunately, the fertilizers that make up a hydroponic formula are not sold as pure nitrogen or pure potassium, so it gets more complex. They are sold as chemical compounds, such as calcium nitrate, potassium nitrate, magnesium sulfate, potassium sulfate and mono potassium phosphate.

Since there are many dependable pre-mix hydroponic formulas available, it is generally more efficient and more economical to use a proven formula that contains all of the above mentioned nutrients in the correct quantities for plant growth.

Whether you are using a pre-mixed formula or creating your own, it is important to follow these guidelines:

1. Weigh or measure the nutrients carefully.
2. Place the nutrients in separate piles or containers to be sure the proportions make sense.
3. Be sure no components are left out or measured twice.
4. Accuracy should be within 5%.

5. When you are sure the proportions are correct, pour your nutrients into the water in the mixing containers and stir vigorously. Nutrients will dissolve best in warm water.
6. Measure the nutrient concentration level and record it.

Table 9.6: Chemicals needed to prepare 1000 litres of nutrient solutions proposed by Dr. Alen cooper

S. No.	Nutrient chemicals	Weight in grams
1.	Potassium dihydrogen phosphate	263.00
2.	Potassium nitrate	583.00
3.	Calcium nitrate	1003.00
4.	Magnesium sulphate	513.00
5.	EDTA iron	79.00
6.	Manganese sulphate	6.10
7.	Boric acid	1.70
8.	Copper sulphate	0.39
9.	Ammonium molybdate	0.37
10.	Zinc sulphate	0.44

HYDROPONIC, ORGANIC AND REGULAR FERTILIZERS

Both hydroponic fertilizer and fertilizer intended for use in soil contain the three major nutrients: Nitrogen, Phosphorus and potassium. The major difference between hydroponic fertilizer and dirt fertilizer is that hydroponic fertilizers contain the proper amounts of all the essential micronutrients that dirt fertilizers do not include, (the plants are expected to find these elements in the soil, assuming that the trace elements are in fact present in the soil). Problems can arise for the plants if any or all of the micro-nutrients are not present in the soil or are depleted by successive (or excessive) plantings. Hydroponic fertilizers are usually in a purer form with fewer impurities than the "dirt" fertilizers so that they are stable and are more water soluble.

Organic fertilizers are very different than either the hydroponic or dirt fertilizer, both in composition and how they deliver the nutrients to the plants. Organic fertilizers rely on the action of bacteria and microbes to break down the material into its basic elements so the plants can use it. The hydroponic and dirt fertilizers supply the plants with these elements *ready-to-use.*

Replacement of Nutrient Solution

A nutrient solution which is recycled through a hydroponic garden must be renewed on average every 4-14 days, or should receive regular nutrient supplements. The life of a solution varies with the nutrient demand of the plants. A solution feeding a bed of seedlings may have a practical life of 3-4 weeks because of the small nutrient usage. By the time the plants reach full maturity and maximum production potential, the solution may need renewing every 4-7 days. In all hydroponic systems it is important that water loss from solutions by evaporation and/or plant transpiration is replaced daily. This can be done manually or automatically with a ball float valve in the nutrient tank. During hot weather, water usage is extremely high and, if not replaced daily, the volume of the remaining solution may become inadequate to maintain the moisture level in the growing medium.

Also, the nutrients become concentrated, and in extreme situations could induce a temporary salinity problem and adversely affect plant growth.

All hydroponic units using a growing media need to be flushed out with water every so often (1-4 weeks). This practice prevents the possible build up of unused salts in the medium to toxic levels.

The changing of the old nutrient also removes root exudates that are naturally produced. In soil, the roots are always seeking a new growing area, so exudates do not build up. Fresh water also helps prevent harmful fungi from growing on the plants roots.

FERTIGATION

Fertigation combines the two main factors of supplying water and plant nutrients that are essential for plant growth. The right combination of the two is the key to obtain high yields and quality produce.

The method of premixing all fertilizer materials in the medium before planting may include the use of slow-release nitrogen materials such as Isobutylidene diurea (IBDU), or sulfur coated urea (SCU). This method is not commonly used but, when compared to the liquid-feed method, it is reported to produce equal or better yields of tomatoes **(Sheldrake *et al.*, 1971)**.

Tissue analysis is the best method to evaluate the nutritional status of the plants and the success of the fertilization program. Periodic sampling and analysis of leaf tissue during growth of the crop will provide information that can be used to make adjustments in fertilizer practices, as well as to help interpret any abnormal plant symptoms. Whole leaves, leaf petioles, or leaf blades are the plants parts normally used, although desirable levels for nutrients vary depending upon the part sampled, its location on the plant, and the analytical methods used. Desirable levels of nutrients have been reported for tomatoes, cucumbers, and a wide range of vegetables **(Ward, 1973; Wittner and Honma, 1979; Lorenz and Tyler, 1983; Johnson, 1980)**.

Methods of Fertigation

Mix the fertilizers required for a particular crop with daily water requirement of that crop and apply manually or through fertigation system. The amounts of fertilizers mixed with irrigation water will vary depending on the crops, crop growth stage and the hydroponics technique used.

However, at all stages of crop growth, the pH of the nutrient solution must be maintained between 6.5 to 8.5 and EC between 1.5 to 2.5 dS/m. For circulating techniques (DFT and NFT), supply the nutrient solution for a predetermined time period. For aggregate systems (solid media culture), fertigation can be done manually or through drip irrigation system. Supply the fertilizers with irrigation water for a predetermined time period so that the water content of the growing media does not increase beyond field capacity. When fertigation is not done, the crop must be irrigated with water to maintain the medium at field capacity.

Advantages of Fertigation

1. Increasing both yield and quality of produce
2. Improving fertilizer use efficiency and reducing leaching below root zone thus minimizing pollution
3. Accurate and uniform application of fertilizers
4. Saving on labour
5. Ability to meet plant nutrient demand under given climatic conditions and during different crop growth stages

Factors to be Considered in Fertigation

1. Growing media
2. Fertilizers used
3. Irrigation water quality

As the first two factors have discussed earlier, only irrigation water quality is discussed here.

Irrigation Water Quality

Use good quality water with its pH and EC suitable for plant growth. Based on pH, EC and soluble salt content, water quality can be divided into 03 classes (Table 9.7). Non-hazardous and medium class water can be used for fertigation. However, when latter is used for fertigation, thoroughly leach the growing medium at least once a year.

Water suitable for hydroponics should have a conductivity less than 500 uS/cm, or a total salt concentration less 300 ppm. Harmful amount of sodium and boron can cause problems in some areas. Very soft water should be used with calcium-containing nutrients. Hard tap water usually works very well, but after pH adjustment may ìbounce back to very high pH values.

A 500 gallon tank feeding trays filled with perlite in. Lettuce and herbs are grown in the tray

With about 15 minutes of daily maintenance per day, an aquaponic system can provide fresh fish and vegetables year-round.

Hydroponic tomatoes grown in perlite.

A 3-bay, controlled environment greenhouse

Hydroponic herbs grown in NFT (Nutrient Film Technique)

Hydroponic lettuce grown in an NFT (Nutrient Film Technique)

Table 9.7: Classification of irrigation water used for hydroponics

Quality factors	Unit	Water quality classes		
		Non-hazardous	Slight to moderate	Severe
pH		Normal range 6.5-8.4		
Salinity Ec	dSm^{-1}	0.00-0.8	0.8-3.0	>3.0
Sodium	me/lit	<3.0	>3.0	-
Chloride	me/lit	<3.0	>3.0	-
Boron	mg/lit	<0.7	0.7-3.0	>3.0
Bicorbonates	me/lit	<1.5	1.5-8.5	>8.5

STANDARD NUTRIENT SOLUTIONS

Premixed nutrient solutions are available from a number of sources. Many solution like bioplantomin and biofert-M are relatively inexpensive and easy to use. As you become more familiar with growing plants hydroponically, you may wish to make your own nutrient solutions. You may also like to observe the effects of varying the nutrient concentrations and to produce specific deficiency symptoms by omitting one nutrient. The effects of changing the total nutrient concentration or the solution pH are also interesting. The nutrient solutions are basically enriched mineral water.

D. R. HOAGLAND STANDARD SOLUTION METHOD

The nutrient solution, developed by D. R. Hoagland at the university of California, can be made from readily available salts that will supply the major elements (macronutrients) needed for plant growth. It is easy to prepare and usually gives satisfactory results. (Table 9.8).

Table 9.8:

Salt	Amount for 25 gallons of solutions
Potassium phosphoate - monobasic (KH_2PO_4)	1/2 ounce or 1 teaspoon
Potassium nitrate (KNO_3)	2 ounces or 4 teaspoon to powdered salt
Calcium nitrate Ca $(NO_3)_2$	3 ounces or 6 teaspoons
Magnesium sulfate($MgSO_4$)	1 1/2 ounces or 3 teaspoons

The salts should be dissolved in warm water separately and then added to the solution tank. Reagent or chemical grade potassium phosphate and magnesium sulfate are recommended. Fertilizer grade potassium nitrate and calcium nitrate may be used and are less expensive than the chemically pure forms.

Micronutrients are needed in extremely small amounts. Because it is difficult to weigh out such small quantities, stock solutions of dilute micronutrients should be made up and added to the solution tank. Use only reagent grade chemicals, which are usually available in hobby shops. If tap water is used, zinc sulfate and copper sulfate may not be required. The small amounts of zinc and sulfur needed are usually present in the water or as an impurity in the other fertilizer nutrients.

Chemical	Amount for 1 gallon of stock solution	Amount of stock solution for 25 gallons of nutrient solution
Boric Acid (H_3BO_3)	2 teaspoons	1/2 pint
Manganese chloride ($MnCl_2.4H_2O$)	1 teaspoon	1/2 pint
Zinc sulfate ($ZnSO_4.7H_2O$)	2 teaspoons	1/2 teaspoon
Copper sulfate ($CuSO_4.5H_2O$)	1 teaspoon	1/2 teaspoon
Iron sulfate ($FeSO_4.7H_2O$)	4 teaspoon	1/2 pint

An iron chelate should be substituted for the iron sulfate if your tap water is alkaline. Mix 1 1/2 ounces of Nafe (III) EDTA (13 percent Fe_2O_3) in 5 quarts of water. Use 1/4 pint of this solution for 25 gallons of stock solution. Further other chelate products calculate the amount required to result in a final nutrient solution containing 1 part per million of elemental Iron.

As the plants take up nutrients they will release chemicals into the solution that may cause it to become more alkaline. When the pH rises above 7.0, add enough sulfuric acid (battery acid) to bring it back to a pH between 5.5 to 6.5. For large plants it may be necessary to add acid daily. If the solution becomes acidic, the pH can be raised with potassium hydroxide (KOH) or sodium hydroxide (NaOH). A variety of pH meters and testing kits are available for checking pH levels.

Note: The nutrient solution should be changed once every two weeks when the plants are small and once a week as the plants begin to grow rapidly. Add water daily to keep the amount of solution constant.

KNOP'S SOLUTION

Calcium nitrate $Ca(NO_3)_2 4H_2O$..........0.8 gram/lt.
Potassium nitrate KNO_3..........0.2 gram/lt.
Magnesium sulfate $MgSO_4.7H_2O$..........0.2 gram/lt.
Iron Phosphate $FePO_4$.......... Traces only

SACH'S SOLUTION

Potassium nitrate (KNO_3)..........0.5 gram/lt.
Calcium Phosphate $(PO_4)_2$..........0.5 gram/lt.
Magnesium sulfate $MgSO_4.7H_2O$..........0.5 gram/lt.
Zinc Chloride ($ZnCl_2$)..........0.25 gram/lt.
Iron sulfate ($FeSO_4$).......... Traces only

HOGLAND SOLUTION

$Ca(NO_3)_2 4H_2O$..........1.8 gram/lt.
KNO_3..........0.51 gram/lt.
KH_2PO_4..........0.14 gram/lt.
$MgSO_4.7H_2O$..........0.49 gram/lt.
Ferric Tartarate..........0.005 gram/lt.

COMBINATION DEVELOPED BY NBRI LUCKNOW FOR VEGETABLES AND FLORICULTURE

Magnesium Sulphate.......... 0.5 gram
Double Superphosphate.......... 0.5 gram
Potassium Nitrate.......... 0.4 gram
Ammonium Sulphate.......... 0.3 gram

THESE COMBINATION ARE DISSOLVED IN 4.5 LITER OF WATER

Non Standard Solutions

Some Non Standard Solution for Experimental Purpose can be made as follows:

Calcium Nitrate.. 1 gram

Potassium Nitrate.. 0.2 gram

Magnesium Sulphate.. 0.2 gram

Ferrous Suphate .... 0.1 gram

Urea.. 0.2 gram

DISSOLVE THIS COMBINATION IN ONE LITER OF WATER

This combination gives best results in seed germination experiments and also provides all essential nutrients and plant growth can be maintained over a long period.

Herbs in General Mixing directions based on teaspoon/10 litre (for small quantities only).

	Veg	Bloom
$Ca(NO_3)_2$	2 1/2	2
K_2SO_4	1/6	1
KNO_3	5/6	None
KH_2PO_4	5/8	3/4
$MgSO_4$	2 3/4	2 7/8
TE	1/5	1/6

A & B concentrate (stock solution) for Mixing directions based on teaspoon/10 litre

Herbs in General Mixing directions based on grams/ ltr (more accurate on a larger volume)

	Veg	Bloom
$CaNO_3$	1.500gr	1.020 gr
K_2SO_4	0.115 gr	0.695 gr
KNO_3	0.522 gr	None
KH_2PO_4	0.348 gr	0.435 gr
$MgSO_4$	1.120 gr	1.212 gr
TE	0.100 gr	0.090 gr

A & B concentrate (stock solution) for Mixing directions based on grams/ltr

A sample hydroponic mixture can be made by dissolving one gram of any NPK (Nitrogen-Phosphorus-Potassium) fertilizer mix in one liter of water. Add enough lime to keep pH of the solution between 6.5 to 7.7. The neutral solution give the best result. This combination work well if the local water contain sufficient iron and magnesium.

Nutrient Solution from Organic Waste:

- A few simple and safer nutrient solution can be prepared from the fully cured cow dung manure, compost and from vermiwash.
- Solution from cowdung manure:
- Take about 200 gram of fully cured cowdung manure.
- Dissolve it in about 500 ml of water and shake it well about 5 to 10 minutes.
- Keep it for an hour to allow the setting of the manure at the bottom.
- Take the strained supernatant and filter it using cotton or filter paper.
- The filtered solution can be used as nutrient solution.
- Concentrate the solution by sun drying method.
- (The potency of the solution will depend upon the quality of the manure. Standardize the solution by appropriate dilution through trial and error method.)
- Solution from the Self-made Compost

How to Make Compost

What is Composting - It is a process of decomposition which involves the conversion of organic substances by micro-organism into utilizable form in the absence or presence of air to yield a sanitary soil supplement. (This supplement will be used to make nutrient solution).

For our purpose of making compost we may use wastes from animals (droppings of cow, goat etc.), vegetables wastes, aquatic weeds, wheat stalks. You may also add synthetic nitrogen, phosphorus and potash fertilizers but not necessary. For our purpose the Heap Composting (Aerobic) method would be ideal.

Tips for Facilitators - In nature all dead organic matter is gradually acted upon by the forces of nature such as sun, wind, rain and microbes, which serve to break-down complex material into simpler molecules. This process of decomposition can be used to convert organic wastes especially vegetables peels from the kitchen and fallen leaves, dead leaves, dry weed, harvest residue, fallen flowers and fruits from the garden, to make compost.

Heap Method:

1. Segregate available organic waste into three types as follows:-
   a) Hard stalks and woody biomass.
   b) Carbon rich soft biomass (straw, vegetables peel etc.)
   c) Nitrogen rich biomass (Fresh grass, weeds, animal feed etc)
2. Arrange the segregate as follows:
   a) All hard stalk and woody biomass are spread to form 15-20 cm thick base for heaps.
   b) A 20 cm thick carbon rich soft biomass.
   c) 10 cm thick nitrogen rich biomass.
   d) Cover the heap to formed (1 - 1.5 m high) with a thin layer of sol or dry leaves.
   e) After 7 - 10 days mix the material thoroughly.

The compost would be ready after 2 - 3 weeks depending upon the environmental temperature.

Solution from Biomanure

(For this you may use your kitchen waste (only green vegetable) to make the biomanure and then can make your nutrient solution. If you use only green vegetable waste, it will be possible to standardize the technique of making the nutrient solution as well. This technique is very simple)

Biodung manure can be prepared in ground-level heaps under a tree shade or on the roof by providing shade to the heap. It does not require any special structure like pit or tank. It is chiefly made from agriculture field biomass, monsoon weed and leaf litter. It requires very little cowdung about 1 to 2% of the weight of the biomass, which is used as microbial inoculum.

Systematic layers as mentioned above is required if different kinds of biomass is used. No such layering is necessary for kitchen green vegetable waste.

The biomass is well soaked in water and cowdung is covered with black polythene sheet. Polythene coverage help in maintaining moisture at 50 - 60% and temperature around 40 – 50°C.

Solution from the Soil

- In nature, fire and water act together to recharge the soil with nutrients. When forest burns, wood turn into ash. Wood ash is rich in potassium, one of the fundamental nutrients for plants. When rain comes, the dead leaves and other fallen branches are helped along their path to decay. The animals and insects hasten this process by their consumption of plants and excretion of organic wastes.
- The organic matter in the soil is biologically decomposed into basic salts. They are in soluble form and absorbed by plants through their roots.

- Here we will make use of this property of these released nutrients (water solubility) for making nutrient solution from soil as follows:
- Collect soil which is rich in organic matter (The soil from forests is ideal, or soil from agriculture field in which agriculture residue was left before the rainy season or top soil called humus, under the tree.)
- Take soil sample (about 350 to 400 grams) in a two-liter plastic transparent jar.
- Add one liter water to it.
- Shake it well for 30 minutes.
- Keep the jar for 2 to 3 hours to allow the setting of undissolved content.
- Take the supernatant and filter it by using cotton / filter paper with the help of a funnel in a transparent bottle.
- Keep the bottle in sunlight (at least 6 to 8 hours) to kill pathogens.
- Standardize the solution by appropriate dilution or concentration.

CHAPTER 10

BIOPLANTOMIN – A SUCCESSFUL MEDIA FOR MODERN HYDROPONICS

Until 1992, the main objective of hydroponic was to grow plants without soil in small spaces, laboratories was use less for most of the farmers in growing crops in open field. Some areas are problematic in India like salt-affected and deserts of arid zone where cultivation of vegetables, cut flowers and other field crops is not possible. In 1992, a major breakthrough in hydroponic development was come when the author of this book Dr. Dharm Singh, a noted agriculture scientist, while working in National Horticultural Research and Development Foundation, invented a formula of preparing a complete liquid plant food, named **Bioplantomin.**

By evolution and standardization of this solution, it become possible to grow plants very successfully in problematic areas of India on a commercial scale. This solution was derived from selected biomass and processed through microbial action and tested on 2780 plants for 3 years from 1993 to 1995. He also tried this solution for raising field crops in problematic fields specially in deserts of Western Rajasthan where plants growing is not possible due to scare availability of water and unproductive pure sands.

WHAT IS BIOPLANTOMIN ?

Bioplantomin is a multi-action complete plant food. It is highly suitable for feeding of a wide range of plant species. It is non toxic and stable nutrient solution of organic nature. It is highly suitable not only for successful modern hydroponics but also can be used in open field by most of the farmers for cultivation of field crops. Bioplantomin has photo hormonal properties for stimulation of seed germination and inducing reproductive growth of plants. It has suppressive effect on fungus, virus and bacterial infestation. It works somewhat similar to the principle of potency effectiveness and its micro-quantity need makes its application cost effective. It contains N, P, K, Ca, Mg, S, Mn, Zn, Fe, B, Mo and Vitamins, herbal enzymatic, herbal hormonal constituents. Its 1 ml dose is recommended to mix in a litre of water in hydroponics.

WHAT IS DESERT-HYDROPONIC ?

It is a technique of growing plants in open field in desert areas using aqua solution in earthen pitchers. This technique is more advantageous for arid regions of India where water is scarcity available and soil are pure sandy and unproductive. This technique of plant growing in deserts referred to as desert hydroponics.

The bioplantomin is used in earthen pitchers @ 1 ml per litre of water. The pitchers filled with water plus bioplantomin is buried in open field at a spacing of 6 x 5 feet. The seedling of vegetables are planted in soil around the pitcher. The spacing between plant to plant depends upon the kind of plant species to be grown. The plants get nutrient and water easily from the soil through seepage / leaching. The tomato, capsicum, watermelon, musklemon, chilly, brinjal, onion, garlic, tulsi, ashwagandha, gladeoli, tuberose, marigold and iris were grown very successfully in deserts of western Rajasthan by this technique.

CHAPTER 11

HYDROPONIC METHODS FOR NURSERY AND ORCHIDS GROWING

NURSERY RAISING

As in open field agriculture, production of vigorous seedlings or planting material of high yielding varieties is an essential step of hydroponics/soilless culture, to obtain economic yields.

REQUIREMENTS FOR NURSERY RAISING

1. Growing Media

The growing medium must provide satisfactory conditions for seed germination and to raise pest and disease free seedlings. A material that is friable, moderately fertile, well drained. have sufficient water holding capacity with good aeration and free from pests and disease causing organisms, must be selected as medium for seed germination or rooting the planting materials. The following materials can be used as medium to raise seedlings or to root planting materials.

- Old coir dust.
- Carbonized rice husk.
- Fine sand or fine sand and old coir dust mixture.
- Rockwool, peat, perlite or vermiculite etc.

Fig. 11.1: Different type of nursery containers.

Sterilize the medium before use. For coir-dust, add hydrated lime to bring its pH to neutral. For a 5 kg coir-dust block, about 100 – 250 g hydrated lime is needed.

Rockwool is most often used in the form of cubes for seed propagation. To plant seeds in rockwool, soak the cube in water or nutrient solution and drop the seed into the hole in the center of the rockwool cube. Many growers seed into rockwool cubes and, when the seedling develops, move the whole cube with the plant in it, into the hydroponic garden. A seedling in a rockwool cube can easily be transplanted into an NFT, ebb and flow or drip system.

2. Nursery Containers / Trays

Use a container that provides the suitable condition for seed germination and also according to crop and cultivation method. Individual containers / growing blocks used are paper pots, plastic pots, clay pots, styrofoam pots, coconut fibre pots, rockwool blocks, sponge blocks. Trays made up of different materials are available for sale in market. Depending on the requirements, trays may be selected.

Fig. 11.2: Different type of nursery trays

3. Moisture

Saturate your growing medium with water or nutrient solution with a pH of 5.5 - 6.5. Be sure to keep the growing medium moist throughout germination. Ideally, the water or nutrient solution should be kept at 75-80°F. This temperature can be easily maintained with a submersible aquarium heater.

Once your plants have germinated, a nutrient solution with a pH of 5.5 - 6.5 and a nutrient concentration of 1800 - 2000 umhos/cm should be fed.

4. Relative Humidity

The higher the relative humidity, the greater the absorption of water by the seed. Ideally, relative humidity should be 70% - 80% in the air around the media and near 100% right around the seed.

5. Ideal Temperatures

Bottom heat is advantageous for propagation. Heated propagation mats are made for this purpose and are often incorporated into incubation chambers and propagation tables.

Providing the ideal ambient temperature for your seeds will encourage quick germination. The optimum germination temperature for different crop is given in Table 11.1

Table 11.1: The optimum germination temperatures for different crops

S. No.	Crop	Optimum temperature for germination
1.	Carrots	86°F
2.	Cucumbers	76°F
3.	Lettuce	76°F
4.	Melons	90°F
5.	Parsley	77°F
6.	Peas	76°F
7.	Radishes	86°F
8.	Tomatoes	78°F

6. Light

The first few days of seed germination (the time prior to the radical root emerging) can take place in the dark. After that time, light must be provided. If proper light is not provided, a plant will grow tall and spindly as it reaches for the light. This is often referred to as "stretching." Young plants will quickly do this. For seedling growth, having at least 500 foot candles of light is required. This can be either natural or artificial light. If artificial light is used, set a timer that turns the light on for 16 hours and off for 8 hours of each day. Plants do need darkness as part of their daily cycle, so do not leave the light on all of the time.

SEED GERMINATION

Thorough cleaning of the pots followed by washing with 10% Calcium or Sodium hypochloride will ensure disease free condition. Place one seed per block filled with growing medium at the correct depth in the pots or trays. Such necessary conditions for seed germination as moisture, temperature, humidity must be provided. Germination trays can be covered with wet papers or cloth to provide adequate temperature for germination until the seeds sprout. Remove these papers at the time of seedling emergence. Maintain the moisture level of the medium at correct level for uniform germination and application of water in the mornings is preferred.

PLANTING MATERIAL PRODUCTION

Vegetative parts separated from mother plants can also be rooted and used as planting materials. Individual containers or trays filled with growing medium are used for rooting these vegetative parts. Select vegetative parts that are free from pests, disease causing organisms and nematodes for propagation. For example, following materials can be used for propagation.

- Strawberry- Plantlets or runners separated from mother plants
- Gerbera- Plantlets separated from mother plants
- Mint- 10 – 12 cm long semi hardwood stem cuttings

NUTRIENT SUPPLY

Nutrient supply is not necessary until the emergence of first two true leaves. Until such time apply only clean water. However, when they unfold, nutrient supply must begin gradually as the growing medium contains very little plant nutrients. The fertilizer mixture meant hydroponic plants could also be used for nursery plants. Diluted nutrient solution can be applied every day or nutrient solution prepared by dissolving 10 g of Albert's mixture in 10 litre of water can applied every other day.

At the early stage, place the trays or pots in shallow containers that is filled with nutrient solution in such a way that the tray's or pots' lower portion is submerged in the solution. The nutrient solution will reach the media through the holes at the bottom of the pots or nursery trays by capillary action. Vegetative parts for propagation planted in individual containers or trays are also placed in shallow nutrient solution containers as seedling trays.

The nutrient solution can also be applied directly to nursery pots after seed germination or sprouting of planting materials. When applying nutrient solution directly to nursery pots, place the pots or trays on a flat plane and pour solution so that it does not come into direct contact with the small plant; at the early stage apply 5-10 ml solution once a day; and when plants grow, 10-25 ml a day once or twice till establishment.

Once the seedlings or planting materials reach the correct size for planting, they can be planted with the medium. Vegetative parts can sometimes be directly established in the hydroponic system.

NURSERY PERIOD

The nursery period varies with the crops (Table 11.2). Select vigorous seedlings with the characteristics for the variety concerned for establishment in hydroponics. Also tissue cultured plants can be established in hydroponics.

Table 11.2: Nursery Period of different crops

S. No.	Vegetables	Nursery period
1.	Tomato	3 - 4 weeks (2-3 true leaves stage)
2.	Cabbage	4 - 5 weeks (3-4 true leaves stage)
3.	Salad cucumber	3 weeks (3-4 true leaves stage)
4.	Lettuce	2 - 3 weeks
5.	Bell Pepper	4 - 5 weeks
6.	Cauliflower	5 – 6 weeks
7.	Chilli	5 – 6 weeks
8.	Brinjal	5 – 6 weeks
9.	Chineses Cabbage	4 – 5 weeks

SPONGE NURSERY TECHNIQUE

Sponge pieces can be used as nursery medium instead of the above mentioned media materials. 2.5 cm cube sponge blocks can be used for this purpose. Place the seeds at the centre in a cut made on the topside of the sponge block.

Fig. 11.3: Sponge Block **Fig 11.4:** Seedling in a sponge block.

Sponge nursery is maintained as other nurseries. Nutrient supply must begin when the first true leaf begin to unfold. Depending on the cultivation method, the seedlings can be planted in hydroponics system with the sponge block intact. The sponge block may be removed with minimum damage to roots when plants begin to grow.

SEMI-HYDROPONIC FOR GROWING ORCHIDS

Semi-hydroponic(s)TM* or semi-hydro, semi-hydro culture, s/h. Form of *passive hydroponics.* A method of growing plants without soil. Instead a practically inert wicking medium transports water and fertilizer to the roots by capillary action. Medium contains a multitude of free air spaces and thus delivers oxygen to the roots.

Even conventional orchid culture can be considered hydroponic in nature. The medium is there primarily for mechanical support, and provides little, if any, nutrition to the plant, that being provided by the nutrient solutions used.

Semi-hydroponic(s)TM popularized and named by Ray Barkalow (First Rays Orchids - [1]) has become a popular method for growing orchids both out- and indoors.

PLANTING

Orchids can be planted in any container (not glass) with - *important-* no drainage holes at the bottom but a few extra holes 3-5 cm up at the sides of the pot. The idea is to provide a water reservoir at the bottom of the container from which the medium wicks moisture to the roots.

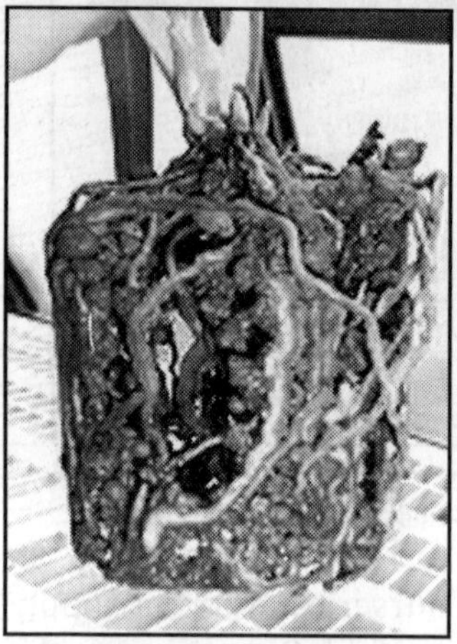

Cattleya transferred to semi-hydro culture 5 weeks earlier. Rich development of surface roots

New growth on *Dendrobium Phalaenopsis* transferred to semi-hydro 6 weeks ago.

Media

LECA (Lightweight Expanded Clay Aggregate) - expanded/fired clay pellets or clay pebbles, perlite, vermiculite, gravel, charcoal, rockwool, coconut husk chips and their combinations.

Water

Medium is flushed with tepid water solution when reservoir is nearly empty. Translucent pot may help to see when it is.

Fertilizer

Orchids are fertilized with 1/2 or 1/4 of recommended strength of balanced inorganic fertilizer with every watering. Container is flushed with plain water every month to prevent harmful salt build up.

Conversion from Conventional Culture to Semi-Hydroponic

Medium is rinsed and soaked overnight. The plant is removed from the old pot and old medium is thoroughly removed from the roots. Rotten roots are cut away and overlong roots are trimmed. All the roots are thoroughly washed in lukewarm water. Some new medium is arranged at the bottom of the new container. The plant is accommodated and more new medium is put around. The pot is gently shaken, more media is put in, more shaking and so on. The pot is flushed with tepid water. The Orchid is placed in the shade with no fertilizer for the following month.

Transplantation

From semi-hydro to semi-hydro is simply transferring the plant with the medium to a new pot and filling with more *presoaked* medium.

Suitable Orchids for Hydroponics

Most popular orchids will more or less thrive in semi-hydro culture: Paphiopedilums, Phragmipediums, Masdevallias, Phalaenopsis, Cattleyas, Cymbidiums, Oncidiums, Dendrobiums, Epidendrums, Miltoniopsis, Pleurothallids and Zygopetalums.

Exceptions would be very big or "thirsty" plants or those whose roots must dry sometimes completely and even those that require dry rest like *Dendrobium nobile.*

Advantages of Semi-Hydroponics

Its simplicity and effectiveness. No guessing about watering and fertilizing, no media decomposition, practically no root rot, healthy plants, fine blooming, no moving parts, low cost, reusable media.

Disadvantages

The main disadvantage can sometimes be the need of more frequent watering, especially when plants begin to fill their pots, are big or otherwise demand lots of water. Obviously, a bigger water pot/reservoir may help (or side holes higher up on the pot). If the sides of the translucent containers receive enough light exposure then algae will grow on the outer layer of the potting media. This is mainly an aesthetic concern and not a big problem indoors.

CHAPTER 12

SOURCE OF LIGHT

There are four basic building blocks on which plant life is based: Light, Water, Nutrition, and Climate. The most common factor that limits plant growth is the light source. In outdoor gardening, light is obviously not a problem; Mother Nature has seen to proper light balance and intensity for healthy plant growth. The responsibility for proper indoor lighting falls on the gardener. If your plants are not furnished enough light of the correct spectrum, they often will be mere shadows of what they could have been, if they grow at all. When you can't rely on Mother Nature to handle the lighting for you, the next best thing is a High-Intensity Discharge (HID) Metal Halide light system.

The factors of growing plants are interdependent and synergistic. The most important of these is light. Growers should start by getting the best possible light their budget can afford. What light is best, depends on the space and situation available. The following techniques are valid for just about any vegetable or herb, such as tomatoes and basil.

LIGHT SPECTRUMS

White light, as it comes from the sun, is composed of waves of red light, through successively shorter waves to violet light. The band of colors that compose the visible spectrum of light (that which we can see) include, starting with the longest rays, red, orange, yellow, green, blue, indigo and violet. The visible spectrum represents only a part of the radiant energy that comes from the sun and only a part of the visible spectrum is effective in photosynthesis.

Wavelengths exist that we our unable to perceive with our eyes. Beyond the red rays are still longer rays called infrared and beyond the violet rays are even shorter rays called the ultraviolet.

The fact that chlorophyll is green to the eye is evidence that some of the blue and red wavelengths of white light are absorbed, leaving proportionally more green to be transmitted, reflected and seen.

Much of the red, blue, indigo and violet wavelengths are absorbed and used in photosynthesis while part of the red and most of the yellow, orange and green are barely used in photosynthesis.

Light deficiency symptoms

1. Plants will stretch and reach toward the light source
2. Stem elongation
3. Plant deformities
4. No fruit set

ARTIFICIAL LIGHTING

If your hydroponic garden is in direct sunlight, the plants should receive adequate amounts of light and absorb the spectrums they need.

In a greenhouse setting, supplemental light is sometimes used to extend the hours of light a plant receives during low light conditions (cloudy weather or short days), and to extend the growing season of a plant. If you are growing in an area with some, but limited sunlight, such as a windowsill, supplemental lighting will be needed.

Any supplemental light is beneficial to increase plant growth and production. The higher the intensity and the broader the spectrum, the greater the benefit.

You can grow in a completely enclosed space with no natural light if you provide all artificial light but there are several drawbacks including the cost of the lights and the energy to run them is high, there may be a compromise of the plants needs if the artificial lighting does not provide the complete light spectrum the plant needs and artificial lighting will not exactly duplicate the spectrum of light the sun provides.

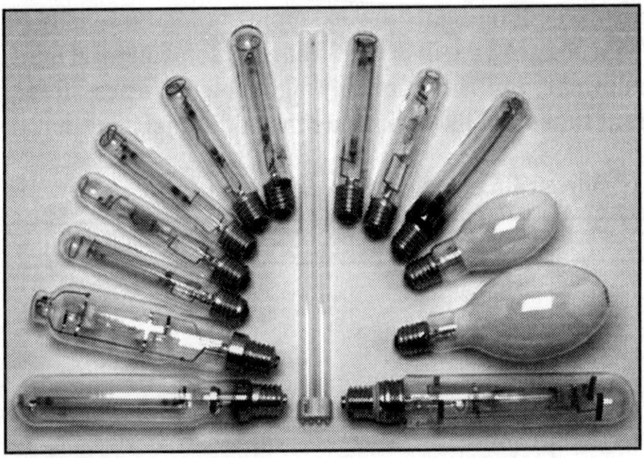

Plant Light Needs

Plants have differing needs for light and, as a general rule, most fruiting crops need more light when they are in a fruiting stage than when they are in a vegetative stage. The chart below shows a variety of crops and their individual light needs.

Lamp Placement

When lighting your plants, the proximity of the lamp to your plants is directly related to the intensity of the light provided. The closer the lamp, the more intense the light. When you raise your lamp, the intensity is lessened. It is important not to have your lamp so close that it burns the plant leaves.

Increased light coverage can be achieved by installing a light mover that will rotate your light. You can also use reflective paint or reflective surfaces (aluminum foil, for instance) surrounding the growing area to increase light.

Types of Lights for Plant Growth

HID (High Intensity Discharge) lights are the common choice for supplemental lighting in a large space such as a greenhouse. They are the most efficient and very intense. Metal halide, mercury vapor and high pressure sodium lights are examples of high intensity discharge lights. If you are growing in an area that has some natural light, such as in a windowsill, you can probably light it with a less intense light. Fluorescent tubes will likely provide the additional light that you need.

Table 12.1: Various crop Light Needs

S. No.	Crop	Light Needs
1.	Beans	Medium - High
2.	Beets	Low
3.	Broccoli	Medium - High
4.	Cabbage	Low -Medium
5.	Carrots	Low
6.	Cauliflower	Medium -High
7.	Cucumber	High
8.	Lettuce	Low
9.	Melons	High
10.	Peas	Medium - High
11.	Peppers	High
12.	Radishes	Low
13.	Onions	Medium - High
14.	Spinach	Low
15.	Tomatoes	High

Fluorescent lights will also be adequate for propagation of seedlings, plant cuttings and some low-light house plants.

In a grow room without noticeable natural light, HID's are necessary to provide ample light for plant production. High Intensity Discharge lights can create an excessive amount of heat.

When using HID's, ventilation and cooling may be necessary. Vented reflector hoods are available for this purpose. Also keep in mind that HID's require high amounts of electricity and are more costly to run than most other types of lights.

Incandescent Light

Although some supplemental light is better than none, incandescent light offers the lowest level of intensity and is generally better used as a room light than a plant light.

Specialty incandescent grow bulbs are available and will provide a better light spectrum than a standard incandescent bulb but the intensity is still limited.

Standard incandescent bulbs are high in the red spectrum but low in the blue spectrum which most plants need for vegetative growth.

Incandescent bulbs are inexpensive to initially buy but they are generally not efficient or effective for plant growth.

Fluorescent Light

Fluorescent tubes offer a broader color spectrum and are available in a variety of kinds including bright white. cool white. warm white. plant bulbs. daylight and full spectrum. The combination of warm and cool white offer a broad light spectrum.

Fluorescent bulbs are relatively inexpensive, long-lasting and provide even, cool lighting.

The down-side to fluorescent lights is that they are low in intensity and need to be very close to the plants to be effective. Seedlings, cuttings and most house plants will benefit from fluorescent lighting.

Metal Halide Light

Metal halide lights offer a broad spectrum with ample blue light for vegetative growth. The metal halides are more efficient than Mercury Vapor lights which at one time were the primary source of HID light.

Metal halides are one of the best light sources for plant growth and, if you were using only one type of light, metal halide would be the best choice.

High Pressure Sodium Light

High pressure sodium lights are very efficient. They are long lasting and strong in the yellow- red spectrums. Their only disadvantage is that they aren't quite strong enough in the blue spectrum for vegetative development.

The high pressure sodium lights are a good choice for flowering plants. The combination of metal halide and high pressure sodium offers the broadest light spectrum and must be used in situations where no natural light is found.

Visible Radiations Required for Photosynthesis

The radiation is the propagation of electromagnetic energy through space. A triumph of physics in the early twentieth century was the realization that light has properties of both particles and waves. A wave is characterized by a **wavelength**, denoted by the Greek letter lambda (λ), which is the distance between successive wave crests. The **frequency**, represented by the Greek letter *nu* (ν), is the number of wave crests that pass an observer in a given time. A simple equation relates the wavelength, the frequency, and the speed of any wave:

$$c = \lambda v$$

where *c* is the speed of the wave-in the present case, the speed of light (3.0×10^8 m s^{-1}). The light wave is a transverse (side-to-side) electromagnetic wave, in which both electric and magnetic fields oscillate perpendicular to the direction of propagation of the wave and at 90° with respect to each other.

Light is also a particle, which we call a **photon.** Each photon contains an amount of energy that is called a **quantum** (plural quanta). The energy content of light is not continuous but rather is delivered in these discrete packets, the quanta. The energy (*E*) of a photon depends on the frequency of the light according to a relation known as Planck's law:

$$E = hv$$

Where *h* is Planck's constant (1.58×10^{-34} cal/s or 6.63×10^{34} J/s).

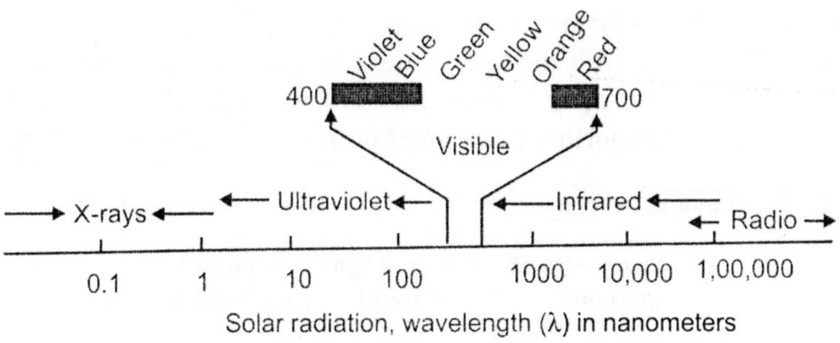

Fig. 12.1: Solar radiation spectrum (λ in μm).

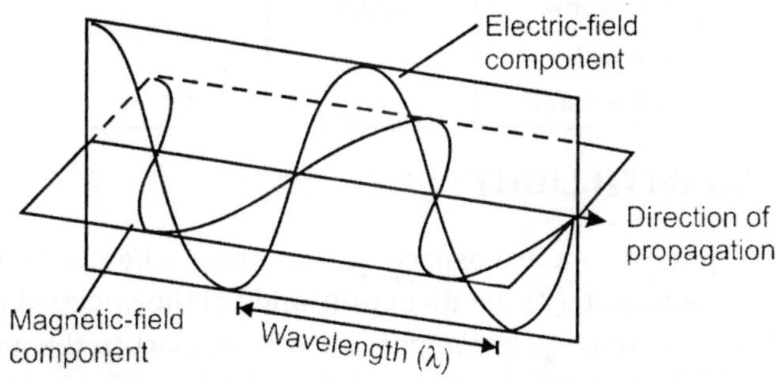

Fig. 12.2: Light is a transverse electromagnetic wave, consisting of oscillating electric and magnetic fields that are perpendicular to each other and perpendicular to the direction of propagation of the light. Light moves at a speed of 3×10^8 m s^{-1}. The wavelength (λ) is the distance between successive crests of the wave.

It is customary in biology to refer to the wavelength of the light wave λ, rather than the frequency κ; the two are related by the simple equation: $\kappa = c/\lambda$. Where *c is* the velocity of light (3×10^{10} cm/s in a vacuum). Therefore, we can consider the energy in a mole of photons, $E = N\kappa\lambda$, where *N* is Avogadro's number [6.02×10^{23} molecules (or photons) per mole]. Thus $E = Nhv = Nhc/\lambda$.

Sunlight is like a *rain of photons* of different frequencies. Our eyes are sensitive to only a small range of frequencies-the visible-light region of the electromagnetic spectrum. Light of slightly higher frequencies (or shorter wavelengths) is in the ultraviolet region of the spectrum, and light of slightly lower frequencies (or longer wavelengths) is in the infrared region. The output of the sun is shown in Fig. 12.3, along with the energy density that strikes the surface of Earth. The absorption spectrum of chlorophyll *a* indicates approximately the portion of the solar output that is utilized by plants.

Table 12.2: Energy of light quanta at different wavelengths

Wavelength of light (nm)	**Colour of light kcl/mol**	**Energy of quanta E_o'v**
350 Ultraviolet	80	35
450 Blue		
550 Yellow	602.6	
650 Red		
750 Infrared	40	1.7

WORKING WITH LIGHT

Three light parameters are especially important when working with light: (1) the **amount**, (2) the **direction**, and (3) the **spectral quality**. The first two parameters are important with respect to the geometry of the part of the plant that intercepts the light. For a flat leaf, a flat or planar light sensor makes sense, and the amount of energy that falls on a flat sensor of known area per unit time is quantified as **irradiance.** Units can be expressed in terms of energy, such as watts per square meter (W m^{-2}). Time (seconds) is contained within the term watt: 1 W = 1 joule (J) s^{-1}. Light can also be thought of as a stream of particles, or **quanta.** In this case, units can be expressed in moles per square meter per second (mol m^{-2} s^{-1}), where *moles* refer to the number of photons (1 mol of light = 6.02×10^{23} photons, Avogadro's number). This measure is called **photon irradiance.**

Quanta and energy units can be inter-converted relatively easily, provided the wavelength of the light is known. The energy of a photon is related to its wavelength as follows:

$$E = \frac{Hc}{\lambda}$$

where *c* is the speed of light (3×10^8 m s^{-1}), *h* is Planck's constant (6.63×10^{-34} J s) and λ is the wavelength of light, usually expressed in nm (1 nm = 10^{-9} m). From this equation it can be shown that a photon at 400 nm has twice the energy of a photon at 800 nm. For simplicity, above can be reduced to the following:

$$E = \frac{1988 X 10^{-19} J}{\lambda}$$

where λ is expressed in nanometers. From this calculation, we can determine that a photon of 400 nm light contains 4.97×10^{-19} *J*.

Now, suppose we have 3 μmol of 400 nm light falling on 1 m^2 every second, or a photon irradiance of 3 μmol m^{-2} s^{-1}. This quantity is approximately the amount of blue light at 400 nm that strikes the surface of Earth on a sunny day. If we want to convert photon irradiance to energy irradiance, we must first convert micromoles to moles (1 μmol = 10^{-6} mol): (3 μmol m^{-2} s^{-1}) × (10^{-6} mol μmol^{-1}) = 3 × 10^{-6} mol m^{-2} s^{-1} of photons, or quanta. Calculating the number of quanta from Avogadro's number gives: (3 × 10^{-6} mol quanta m^{-2} s^{-1}) x (6.02 x 10^{23} quanta mol^{-1}) = 1.8 × 10^{18} quanta m^{-2} s^{-1}. As we already calculated, each photon, or quantum, of 400 nm light contains 4.97 × 10^{-19} *J*. Thus (4.97 x 10^{-19} J $quantum^{-1}$) x (1.8 × 10^{18} quanta m^{-2} s^{-1}) = 0.9 J s^{-1} m^{-2}. Since 1 J s^{-1} = 1 W, therefore, the irradiance will be of 0.9 W m^{-2}.

Turning our attention to the direction of light, light can strike a flat surface directly from above or it can strike the surface obliquely. When light deviates from perpendicular, irradiance is proportional to the cosine of the angle at which the light rays hit the sensor. Thus, irradiance is maximal when light strikes a surface directly from above, and it decreases as light becomes more oblique- similar to the situation with a typical leaf. Sensors that correct for the angle of incidence of light are said to be *cosine corrected*. But there are many examples in nature in which the light-intercepting object is not flat (e.g., complex shoots, whole plants, chloroplasts). In addition, in some situations light can come from many directions simultaneously (e.g., direct light from the sun plus the light that is reflected upward from sand, soil, or snow). In these situations it makes more sense to measure light with a spherical sensor that measures light omnidirectionally (from all directions). The term for this omnidirectional measurement is **fluence rate (Rupert and Letarjet**

1978), and this quantity can be expressed in watts per square meter (W m^{-2}) or moles per square meter per second (mol m^{-2} s^{-1}). It is obvious from the units whether light is being measured as energy (W) or as photons (mol). In contrast to a flat sensor, a spherical sensor is equally sensitive to light, independent of direction. Depending on whether the light is collimated (rays are parallel) or diffuse (rays travel in random directions), values for fluence rate versus irradiance can be quite different from one another. They are equivalent only under special conditions.

Photosynthetically Active Radiation (PAR)

Photosynthetically active radiation (PAR, 400 to 700 nm) may also be expressed on the basis of energy (W m^{-2}) or quanta (mol m^{-2} s^{-1}) (**McCree 1981**). It is important to note that PAR is an irradiance-type measurement. In research on photosynthesis, when PAR is expressed on a quantum basis, it is given the special term **photosynthetic photon flux density (PPED)**. However, it has been suggested that the term *density* be discontinued (**Holmes et al. 1985**) because within the International System of Units (*Systeme Internationale d'Unites*, or SI units) *density* can mean area or volume. Moreover, area is contained within the term flux. PPED has in some cases been shortened to PPF, but it is not clear whether this abbreviation represents an irradiance-type or a spherical measurement. When light moves through water such as lakes or oceans, it scatters in such a way that its direction of travel is randomized. Thus, aquatic photosynthetic organisms can receive light simultaneously from above, below, and the sides. In oceanography and limnology, the light that travels from the water surface toward the bottom is called *downwelling irradiance*, and the light that travels in the reverse direction is called *upwelling irradiance*.

Before the advent of specialized light meters suitable for plant physiology, light was measured in **lux** or **foot-candles**. These measurements are based on the perception of light by the human eye, which is maximally sensitive to light within the green at 555 nm. Sensitivity falls off on both sides of this wavelength and approaches zero within the blue and red, wavelength regions that are important for photosynthesis. Thus, lux and foot-candles are of little use in plant physiology. These units can be converted to the units of irradiance and fluence rate, but only if detailed knowledge about the spectral quality of the light is available, something that can be obtained only by use of an instrument called a *spectroradiometer*, which measures the amount of light at each wavelength.

How much light is there on a sunny day and what is the relationship between PAR irradiance and PAR fluence rate? Under direct sunlight, PAR irradiance and fluence rate are both about 2000 μmol m^{-2} s^{-1}, though higher values can be measured at high altitudes. The corresponding value in energy units is about 400 W m^{-2}. When light is completely diffused, irradiance is only 0.25 times the fluence rate.

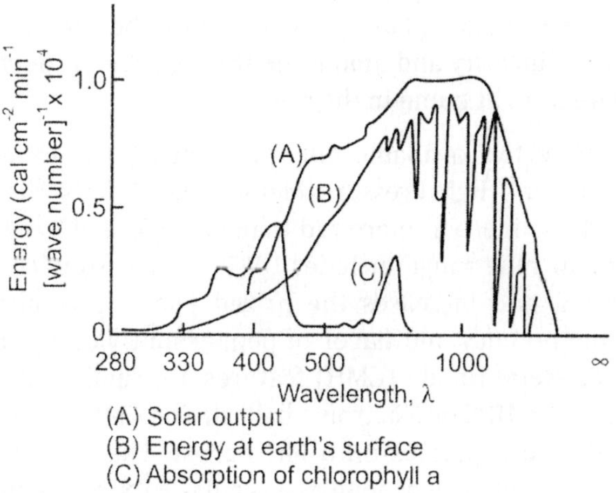

Fig. 12.3: The solar spectrum and its relation to the absorption spectrum of chlorophyll. Curve A is the energy output of the sun as a function of wavelength. Curve B is the energy that strikes the surface of Earth. The sharp valleys in the infrared region beyond 700 nm represent the absorption of solar energy by molecules in the atmosphere, chiefly water vapor. Curve C is the absorption spectrum of chlorophyll a, which absorbs strongly in the blue (about 430 nm) and the red (about 660 nm) portions of the spectrum. Since the green light in the middle of the visible region is absorbed only weakly, much of it is therefore reflected into our eyes and gives plants their characteristic green color. Note that curve C has absorbance rather than energy units.

Conventional wisdom dictates that the growth phase be illuminated by a quartz metal halide (for blue light), the bloom phase by a high pressure sodium (for yellow/orange light). However, a full spectrum is needed for all phases for a variety of functions. Blue induces growth hormones and rooting and reduces stem elongation. Red induces flowering hormones, and provides energy for growth of flowers and leaves. Using only quartz halide during growth phase results in slow growth due to less red light. Using only hps light during the flowering stage often causes leaf yellowing, (due to lack of growth hormones) and often causes stem elongation.

Red light is the most efficient monochromatic spectrum for plant growth. However, all the colors have functions. If a person were especially good at hearing bass sound, that means the other pitches should be emphasized, so that you can hear the whole melody. For light to be efficient for plant growth, it must be full spectrum with close to equal linearity and amplitude through the production of 400-700 nm, with a slight bump in the red.

The best widely available full spectrum light is called "Ceramic Metal Halide" or "High Pressure Metal Halide". This has more blue than a quartz halide, and more red than an HPS, so it's the best for all stages. The far blue range includes UV-B, similar to what is found at high altitudes, and increases the prized phenolic compounds. This increases the potency and flavor of peppermint, licorice, pepper, etc. The Ceramic Metal Halide (CMH) features a ceramic arc tube like an HPS, and uses an HPS or electronic ballast. The CMH is superior to the retro-fit HPS that operates on a MH ballast. The retro-HPS is more expensive, lasts only half as long as a regular HPS, has reduced output, and the spectrum isn't as good as CMH. The retro-quartz-halide that operates on an HPS ballast is very inefficient.

A mixture of halide and sodium is sometimes recommended. Mixing the two different light sources is difficult unless the horizontal orientation is used, and even then, the light under the halide is more halide (and the light under the HPS is more HPS). Halide and HPS light waves are out of phase with each other, and like oil and water, don't fully blend together. The quartz metal halide doesn't operate very well horizontally, the light is less total, doesn't reflect as well and bulb life is shortened. However, quartz halide and hps can be blended by having both in the same reflector and spinning the reflector.

Light Distribution

Around the edge of a cluster of horizontal lights is weak diagonal lighting; this can be compensated for by 100 w side lights. If a single horizontal light were used, non-uniform growth would result from the non-uniform distribution of light. For a single light, a paraboloid reflector would give uniform distribution of lighting. However, a cluster of full spectrum horizontal lights is the best:

Table 12.3: Average Lumen Per Watt Output of Common Lamps

100 Watt Light Bulb	17.5 Lumens per watt
40 Watt Fluorescent Tube	22 lumens per watt
1000 Watt Metal Halide	125 lumens per watt.
1000 Watt High Pressure Sodium	140 lumens per watt

- Full spectrum light sources would be in phase with each other.
- Light directly from the bulb has more energy than reflected light.

Overlapping of light patterns increases total light due to the array effect (that's why chandeliers have many instead of one big candle) allows for sufficient light in fringe areas, at edges of most light footprints increases diffusion because light comes from different angles; this increases reception of light by the leaf surface.

The array effect enhances light output by 20% when two or more lights are separated (but close) and whose light rays collide with each other. If the lights aren't aimed at each other, an array effect will still be gained with a diffuse reflective surface.

A horizontal 400 w CMH full spectrum light, with a horizontal paraboloid diffuse reflector, covers about a three foot x four foot oval area by itself. When combined in a cluster, each such light covers about a four foot x five foot area. This is because outside the three foot x four foot area of high intensity, there is a fringe area of lesser intensity. When the fringe areas overlap, they become high intensity areas.

The highest reflective surface is 98% reflective, and this is specular or mirror-like. The specularity reflects light at exact angles, like the edges of a pool table. This has the disadvantage of creating hotspots (unless the angles are very well-designed and precisely shaped, as in a four foot parabolic reflector). The lack of diffusion or multiple angles of light rays can create shadows on the leaf surface.

The leaf receives better when light is coming from different angles, so I recommend the bulb be oriented horizontally, with a diffuse reflective surface. When horizontal lights are in a cluster, the different angles of light increase diffusion. White is diffused, and the best white paint is about 90% reflective. Glossy white is only 68% reflective. Some types of flat white can't always be cleaned, but can be repainted. Silver reflective surfaces are normally specular, but there is a 97% reflective silver that has micro indentations for diffusion.

High-Intensity Discharge (HID)

It is hard to compare HID lights with fluorescent tubes or incandescent light bulbs. Although they each create light from electricity, that's where the similarity ends. Fluorescent tubes emit a gentle, low temperature light in a very low wattage. Excellent for the first two weeks of most any plant's life, fluorescent lights simply do not provide the intensity of light required for most vegetables, flowers and ornamentals. Incandescent lights ('regular' light bulbs) are even worse for horticulture because they are very expensive to operate, put off as much heat as light, and do not offer the spectrums of light required for healthy plant growth. Even when incandescent light bulbs are altered with interior coatings to change their spectrum (like the "grow light" bulbs you see in the grocery store), they still do not come close to providing the kind of light a plant needs for robust, active growth. The only thing that will really grow and prosper under an incandescent grow bulb is your electric bill!

HID lighting systems represent the safest, most economical way of providing light for your plants. They are used all the time in parking lots, warehouses, baseball diamonds, football fields and other places where reliability and economy are a prime concern. Systems used for garden lighting are constructed differently, but the features of dependability and cheap operation remain the same. Two common types of **HID** lighting have been adapted for safe use in the garden and greenhouse:

Metal Halide

Metal Halide light produces an intense light of a blue-white spectrum excellent for vegetative plant growth. Geraniums, marigolds, mums, zinnias, and violets all thrive under Metal Halide light, as do most vegetables. A plant grown under a halide light will often exhibit increased leaf growth, and strong stem and branch development. Roses grow hearty under metal halides, and seem to burst with buds before flowering time. A wonderful general purpose garden light, if your garden is to have only one light source, metal halide will be your best choice.

High-Pressure Sodium (HPS)

High-Pressure Sodium (HPS) light puts off an orange: shaded light which simulates the rich red hue of the autumn sun. Best as fruiting or flowering lights, the HPS systems are often used In conjunction with metal halide for a complete balance of light spectrum in the garden. Flowers and vegetables finished off under HPS will show tighter, stouter blossoms with increased yields. HPS lights are commonly used In commercial greenhouses as starting lights and for supplemental light for off-season crops. Some types of plants respond particularly well to HPS lighting, such as the herbs dill and coriander.

ELECTRONIC BALLASTS

Electronic ballasts are more efficient than magnetic, and also improve bulb life and efficiency. Be sure to get an e-ballast that is protected against electromagnetic interference (emi). Life Lights is protected against emi, as required by FCC regulations, and is German VDE-listed. The electronic ballast also improves the spectrum; the spikes are smoothed out. CMH, whether powered by electronic or magnetic ballasts, is a full spectrum light - the best for SAD (seasonal affective disorder) or horticultural applications.

Different E-Ballasts such as Life Lights

- Have long-range ignitors (up to 90'); magnetic ballasts typically have short-range ignitors (up to five feet); and most e-ballasts are only rated for 12' of lamp wire.

- Have 6 KV pulse-rated wire and quick disconnect connectors, including a ground wire. Others may have only two bare non-pulse-rated wires sticking out of the ballast enclosure (with no strain relief), or have connectors that could melt.
- Had only two percent failure rate in VDE destructive halt tests, and had a 0% failure rate in tests of normal operation done by BC Hydro Power.
- Have US patents for their advanced technology.
- Sealed, and cooling fans pull air by the heat sink instead of the delicate circuits. If not sealed, the circuit would accumulate dust and moisture.
- Have a high frequency carrier wave, not detected by power company detectors. This high frequency simulates natural sunlight, leading to greater absorption of light by the leaf.
- Have three indicator lights to tell if the bulb needs to be replaced or if the lights are dimmed. During cloud cover (in a greenhouse), lights would be at full intensity; if the room were too hot, the lights would be dimmed.
- They are micro-processor-controlled, to adapt quickly to changing circuit conditions, and allow for dimming.

CHAPTER 13

TRAINING AND PRUNING

In hydroponics, the growing medium does not provide enough anchorage as soils. This is more so in liquid cultures as no planting medium is used. Therefore, growers must provide artificial supporting structures and train plants along those structures. Support is especially important, when tall growing indeterminate type crop varieties (tomatoes, cucumber, etc.) or crops bearing relatively heavy fruits (bell pepper, egg plant, etc.) are used in hydroponics.

A polythene string can be tied at the base of each plant using a plastic plant clip or by a loose non-slip knot and the string is tied vertically to the overhead horizontal support to hold the plants. When plants grow, wind the main stems loosely around the string for support. In the case of tall growing indeterminate tomato varieties, placing additional plant clips every 3rd to 4th nodes will be necessary to prevent the plants from slipping down.

For salad cucumbers, the vertical string is attached to each plant with plastic plant clips or by a loose non-slip knot at the base. As the plants grow, wind the main stem loosely around the string for support. Additional plant clips are attached to prevent plants from slipping.

Tall growing indeterminate type tomatoes are trained to a single stem. All lateral branches are removed when they are about 5 cm long. Prune the lateral branches every 3 to 4 days, and it is best done early in the day.

Indeterminate type tomato plants that produce long term crops are lowered to a working height as they grow, keeping production limited to fruit grown on the 2 – 2.5 m of the main stem. When plants grow taller, remove about 04 leaves at the bottom and untie the string from the overhead horizontal support and lower the plants about 60 cm and tie the string shifting to a side. This must be done every 2 weeks, and the strings must be long enough to permit lowering during the entire cropping period

Tomatoes produce large number of fruits at each cluster. To get large, quality fruits, fruit thing will be necessary. Depending on the size required, 3 to 5 fruits may be left in a cluster. For salad cucumbers, umbrella system of pruning can be adopted. It involves pruning all lateral branches until the plant reaches the overhead horizontal support. There, the terminal bud is removed and two side branches are allowed to grow downwards. Vigorous plants will continue to produce fruits.

Salad cucumber may produce more than one fruit per node; these can be thinned out to one fruit per node or allowed to develop if they are not curved or otherwise distorted in shape. Heavy fruiting at lower part of the vine will reduce higher production.

CHAPTER 14

MANAGEMENT REQUIREMENTS OF HYDROPONICS

To develop and maintain a successful hydroponics / soil-less cultivation of crops, meet the following requirements:

1. Maintain the pH of the nutrient solution in the range of 5.8 to 6.5, and electrical conductivity (EC) in the range of 1.5 to 2.5 dSm^{-1}, as these ranges are suitable for plant growth. Any pH or EC outside these ranges will reduce availability and uptake of nutrients and will also damage plant roots.
2. Plants are the best indicators of the nutrient availability. Look for nutritional disorder symptoms in plants and adjust nutrient solution accordingly.
3. Maintain adequate solution temperature. As the temperature goes up, plant respiration increases causing a higher demand for oxygen. At the same time, the solubility of oxygen decreases. This requirement is more critical in green houses and net houses where the temperature is bound to increase during mid afternoons. Steps must be taken to counter such increase.
4. Always ensure that there is plenty of dissolved oxygen in the nutrient solution as the plant roots absorb oxygen. Lack of oxygen will reduces up take of nutrients and thereby the yield and also causes root rot. In closed systems, if the recollected solution is

allowed to fall into the solution tank from a height, natural aeration will take place.

5. In root dipping techniques, maintain adequate air space above the nutrient solution in the container as success depends on the rapid growth and quantity of roots that are exposed to the air. These roots absorb oxygen for the plants. Ideally, top two thirds of the young root system must be in the air and the rest must be floating in the nutrient solution.

6. Avoid any sudden changes in nutrient solution concentration as it can result in unsuitable pH and EC.

7. In root dipping techniques, during crop growth, when the solution level in the container goes down, the ion concentration may increase. Such increase is detrimental to plant growth. If this condition is observed, siphon out the remaining solution and refill with fresh solution.

8. Ensure adequate light for the hydroponics/ soil-less culture plants. Light and all other requirements are the same as though grown in open fields.

9. Always use pest and disease free seedlings and planting materials for establishment of hydroponics crops. Remove and destroy any infected plants as soon as they are found.

10. If nematode problem is observed in solid media culture, discard the plants and sterilize the growing medium. If in doubt, discard and replace the medium. Also ensure that he water supply is also free from nematodes.

11. Algae can build up in the system and block the small tubes used for the delivery of nutrient solution. Use black colour tubes to avoid such problems. Between crops, thoroughly clean the system using a mild solution of chlorine. After cleaning, thoroughly flush the system with fresh water before replanting.

12. Adequate spacing is necessary for plant growth and when vine crops are grown, supports must be provided.

13. In open aggregate techniques, there is a possibility for nutrients to leach when water is applied. Therefore nutrient solution may be

applied continuously instead of water to supply both water and nutrients.

14. If any of these conditions are not fulfilled, one cannot obtain economical yields.

CARE AND MAINTENANCE OF HYDROPONIC SYSTEMS RECIRCULATING SYSTEMS

As the level in the supply tank falls in hydroponic systems which recirculate the nutrient solution, it should be topped off to its original level with water. This can be achieved manually or automatically by the use of a float valve placed in the nutrient tank. Do not top off the tank with nutrient solution, otherwise you will have no idea of its strength.

After a while, the nutrient solution will need replacing. As a rough guide this should be done about every 1-2 weeks in summer, every two weeks in spring and autumn, and in winter every four weeks. As a more accurate method of determining when to replace the nutrient solution, a conductivity meter can be used. This instrument measures the electrical conductivity of freshly prepared nutrient solution, so when the conductivity falls to two-thirds of the original reading, the solution needs to be replaced or topped off with nutrients.

NON-RECIRCULATING SYSTEMS

In systems where the nutrient solution is not recovered and reused, the supply tank is simply topped off with nutrient solution at any convenient time. Make sure that the supply tank is big enough to hold sufficient nutrient solution to last a number of days. Try to keep wastage to a minimum by learning how much is required under various conditions and efficiently applying the correct amount.

MOISTURE CONTENT

The nutrient solution should be applied at a rate to fully wet the growing medium and cause some drainage. Do not keep the growing medium flooded with solution as this will force the exclusion of air and have detrimental effects.

FLUSHING

Over a long period of time, deposition of nutrient salts in the growing medium occurs, which may cause an imbalance in the nutrient supply. Every 1-4 weeks flush the whole system out with plain water.

HIGH TEMPERATURE

If the temperature becomes too hot in summer then some protection will be needed. The plants may need some shelter such as shade cloth if grown outdoors.

If grown inside a greenhouse, shade cloth or the application of whitewash may be needed. In greenhouses, good air movement is essential and will assist growth and reduce the incidence of fungal diseases on the foliage.

LOW TEMPERATURES

Complete protection from low temperatures can only be achieved with a heated and regulated greenhouse. Very little protection can be given to plants grown in the open. Covering plants with a plastic sheet can protect against light frosts, and advance their growth slightly.

CONTAINERS

When building any hydroponic systems, use inert materials like plastic or fiberglass. Some materials corrode and cause a nutrient imbalance. For example, if galvanized iron is used, zinc toxicity in plants will occur.

CHAPTER 15

PROBLEMS OF HYDROPONICS AND THEIR REMEDIES

As experienced in normal crop husbandry, pests and diseases too affect hydroponic plants and they also show physiological as well as nutritional disorders under unfavourable conditions.

Sudden changes in environmental factors, incorrect nutrition supply or irrigation can bring about physiological disorder symptoms in plants. Some crop varieties are more prone to these conditions than others. These problems has been discussed in this chapter.

INSECT-PEST AND DISEASE PROBLEM

In hydroponics, soil borne diseases are virtually eliminated. Certain common pests and diseases however, can affect these plants. Vigilance and early identification are important in controlling such problems. Keep the environment of the hydroponics plants clean and adopt correct cultural practices such as supply of well-balanced nutrients to maintain the plants healthy. Pests and diseases less affect healthy plants. Always start the cultivation with healthy seedlings/planting materials.

Adopt Integrated Pest Management (IPM) strategies recommended for vegetables. If necessary apply recommended chemicals to control insect pests or diseases and always strictly adhere to recommended pre-harvest intervals.

PHYSIOLOGICAL DISORDERS

Sudden changes in environmental factors, incorrect nutrition supply or irrigation can bring about physiological disorder symptoms in plants. Some crop varieties are more prone to these conditions than others.

Blossom End Rot of Tomato

At the bottom end of tomato fruits, brown, sunken leathery spots appear (Fig. 15.1). Calcium deficiency, dry growing medium, sudden supply of water and salt accumulation in root zone are some causal factors. Avoiding these conditions will prevent blossom end rot.

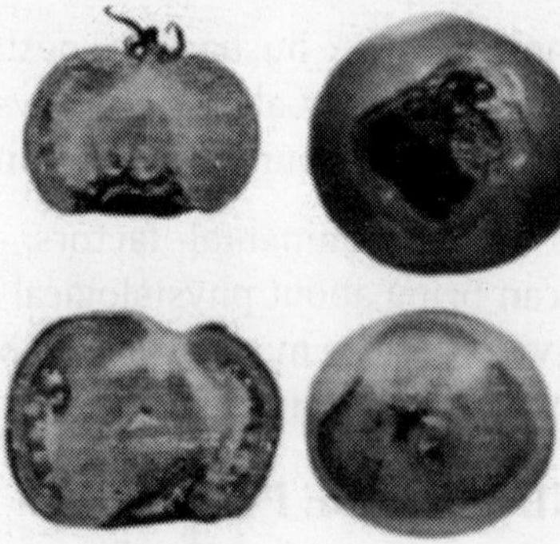

Fig. 15.1: Blossom end rot of tomato

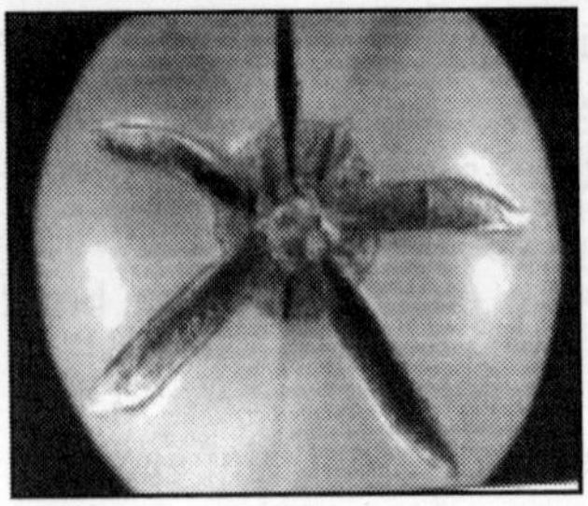

Fig. 15.2: Concentric fruit cracking of tomato

Concentric Fruit Cracking of Tomato

Concentric cracks appear around the fruit stalk (Fig. 15.2) or cracks extending from fruit stalk (Fig. 15.3) appear. High day temperatures, large differences between day and night temperature and sudden change in moisture contents of growing media are major causes of this condition.

Shrink Cracks of Bell Pepper

Shrink cracks appear commonly around the fruit shoulders. Rapid evaporation of condensed moisture on fruit surface causes shrink cracks. Gradual change from day to night temperatures and night ventilation can prevent this condition.

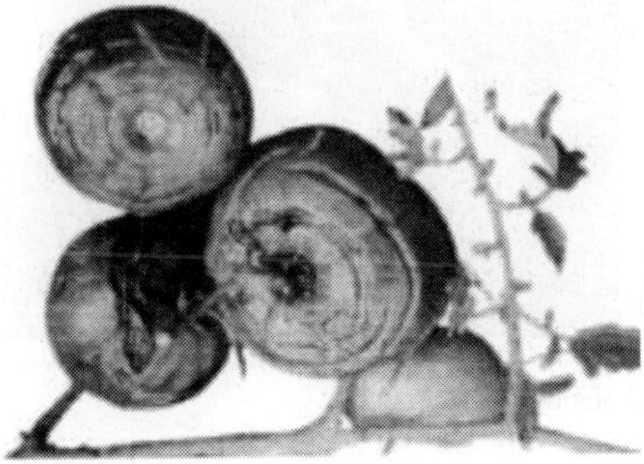

Fig. 15.3: Cracks extending from stalk

Fig. 15.4: Shrink cracks of bell pepper

Fruit Crooking of Cucumber

Fruit crooking is a serious physiological disorder in cucumber. The curvature, known as fruit crooking, begins at early stages of fruit development and may be caused by adverse temperature, excessive moisture in growing medium, poor nutrition, excessive fruit load or insect damage. Affected fruits must be removed as soon as noticed.

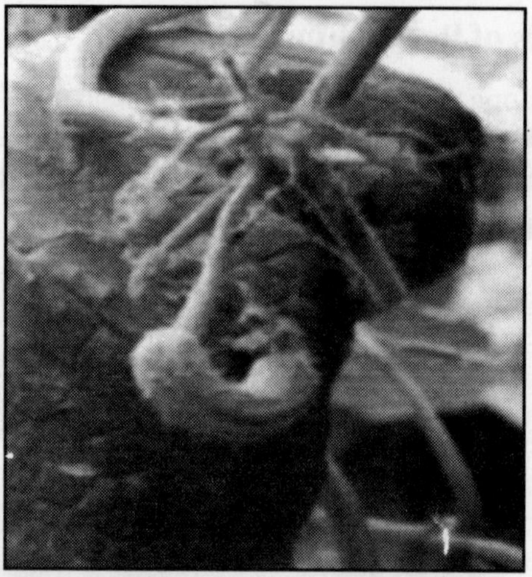

Fig. 15.5: Fruit crooking of cucumber

NUTRITIONAL DISORDERS

In hydroponics all the essential nutrients are supplied through the nutrient solution. If the solution is deficient or excess (toxic) in any of these nutrients or the pH or the EC of the solution is beyond the suitable range, the plants will show nutritional disorder symptoms.

These symptoms include changes in growth rate, size of plants, leaf shape and colour, leaf thickness, stem colour, inter node distance, nature of root system, etc. In addition, fruiting characteristics may change. Although these external symptoms vary according to crops and varieties, some common symptoms are described in appendix I, II.

APPENDIX I

IMPORTANT PLANT DISEASES AND THEIR SYMPTOMS

SN	Disease	Symptoms
1.	Die back	The plant organ dies from top to bottom. This is due to fungus.
2.	Damping off	The plant dies due to rotting off the stem near the soil / water / sand / stone surface
3.	Wilting	The leaf and other part of the plant loose their turgidity and drop. As a result plant topples down. This is due to virus and bacteria.
4.	Blight	Blight means a burnt appearance of leaf, shoot and flower of the whole plant which ultimately leads to death of infected part / plant as the case may be
5.	Exudation	When plant get injury / cut they may get infection. Secretion of fluid from infected plant is known as exudation or bleeding. This is due to bacterial infection.
6.	Dwarfing	There is improper growth and general reduction in the size of leaf stem and other organs due to subnormal growth. Crowding of leaves in the form of rosette is due to failure of the internodes to elongate. Due to micronutrient deficiency (Zn). This is due to virus.
7.	Mosaic	When the chlorophyll is not distributed evenly causing green and yellow area on leaves and gives the appearance of variegated leaf. Mostly in

SN	Disease	Symptoms
		vegetables [Bhindi (ladies finger)].
8.	Vein clearing	The veins are site of vital movement and become colourless. This is due to virus.
9.	Rot	When the effected part / tissue disintegrated the symptom is known as rot. It may be dry or soft rot.
10.	Gall and Tumors	These are due to abnormal development of infected part. Tumors are large and fleshy, irregular in shape and of different colours. Rot knot (gall) is caused by nematodes, white in colour and tumors are caused by bacteria, brown in colour.

APPENDIX II

NUTRITIONAL DEFICIENCY SYMPTOMS IN PLANTS

SN	Nutrient	Deficiency Symptoms
1.	Nitrogen (N)	Growth is restricted and plants are generally yellow (chlorotic) from lack of chlorophyll, especially older leaves. Younger leaves remain green longer. Stems, petioles and lower leaf surfaces of tomato can turn purple.
2.	Phosphate (P)	Plants are stunted and often a dark green colour. Anthocyanin pigments may acumulate. Deficiency symptoms occur first in mature leaves. Plant maturity is often delayed.
3.	Potassium (K)	Symptoms first visible on older leaves. In dicots, these leaves are initially chlorotic but soon scattered dark necrotic lesions (dead areas) develop. In many monocots, the tips and margins of the leaves die first.
4.	Zinc (Zn)	Reduction in internode length and leaf size. Leaf margins are often distorted or puckered. Sometimes intervienal chlorosis.
5.	Iron (Fe)	Pronounce intervienal chlorosis similar to that caused by magnesium deficiency but on the younger leaves.
6.	Boron (B)	Symptoms vary with species. Stem and root apical meristems often die. Root tips often become swollen and discoloured. Internal tissues sometimes

SN	Nutrient	Deficiency Symptoms
		disintegrate (or discolour) (e.g. "heart rot" of beets). Leaves show various symptoms including thikening, brittle-ness, curling, wilting, and chlorotic spotting.
7.	Sulphur (S)	It not often encountered. Generally yellowing of leaves, usually first visible in younger leaves.
8.	Copper (Cu)	Natural deficiency is rare. Young leaves often become dark green and twisted or misshapen, often with necrotic spots.
9.	Calcium (Ca)	Bud development is inhibited and root tips often die. Young leaves are affected before old leaves and become distorted and small with irregular margins and spotted or necrotic areas.
10.	Molybdenum (Mo)	Often intervienal chlorosis devel-oping first on older or midstem leaves, then progressing to the youngest (similar to nitrogen deficiency). Sometimes Marginal scoching or cupping of leaves.
11.	Magnesium (Mg)	Intervienal chlorosis which first develops on the older leaves. The chlorosis may start at leaf margins or tip and progress inward intervienally.
12.	Manganese (Mn)	Initial symptoms are often intervienal chlorosis on younger or older leaves depending on species. Necrotic lesions and leaf sheding can develop later.
13.	Chorine (Cl)	Wilted leaves which then become chlorotic and necrotic, eventually attaining a bronze colour. Roots become stunted and thikened near tips.

APPENDIX III

NUTRITIONAL TOXICITY SYMPTOMS IN PLANTS

SN	Nutrient	Toxicity Symptoms
1.	Nitrogen (N)	Plants usually dark green in colour abundant foliage but usually with a restricted root system. Flowering and seed production can be retarded.
2.	Phosphate (P)	No primary symptoms yet noted. Sometimes copper and Zinc deficiency occurs in the presence of excess Phosphorus.
3.	Potassium (K)	Usually not excessively absorbed by plants. Exess potassium may lead to magnesium deficiency and possible manganese, zinc or iron deficiency.
4.	Zinc (Zn)	Excess zinc commonly produces iron chlorosis in plants.
5.	Iron (Fe)	Not often evident in natural conditions. Has been observed after the application of sprays where it appears as necrotic spots.
6.	Boron (B)	Yellowing of leaf tip followed by progressive necrosis of the leaf beginning at tip or margins and proceeding toward midrib.
7.	Sulphur (S)	Reduction in growth and leaf size. Leaf symptoms often absent or poorly defined. Sometimes intervienal yellowing or leaf burning.
8.	Copper (Cu)	Reduced growth followed by symptoms of iron chlorosis, stunting, reduced branching, thickening and abnormal darkening of rootlets.

SN	Nutrient	Toxicity Symptoms
9.	Calcium (Ca)	No consistent visible symptoms. Usually associated with excess carbonate
10.	Molybdenum (Mo)	Rarely observed. Tomato leaves turn golden yellow.
11.	Magnesium (Mg)	Very little information available on visual symptoms.
12.	Manganese (Mn)	Some times chlorosis, uneven chlorophyll distribution. Reduction in growth.
13.	Chorine (Cl)	Burning or firing of leaf tip or margins. Bronzing, yellowing and leaf abscission and sometimes chlorosis. Reduced leaf size and lower growth rate.

APPENDIX IV

SUITABLE PLANTS FOR HYDROPONICS

S. No.	Common Name	Botanical Name
FOLIAGE PLANTS		
1.	Diffenbachia	*Diffenbachia sp.*
2.	Pendanus	*Pendanus adoratissium*
3.	Syngonium	*Syngonium podophyllum*
4.	Sansveria	*Sansveria trifasciate*
5.	Aglonerna	*Aglonerna commutatum*
6.	Croton	*Codiaeum variegatum*
7.	Cordyline	*Cordyline terminalis*
8.	Zebrina	*Tradescantia*
9.	Albicans	*Polyscias balfouriana*
10.	Coleus	*Coleus blumei*
11.	Caladium	*Caladium hartulanum*
12.	Acalypha	*Acalypha indica*
13.	Altermanthera	*Altermanthera bettzickiana*
14.	Chlorophytum	*Chlorophytum comosum*
15.	Callisis	*Callisia repens*
16.	Banyan	*Ficus benghalensis*
17.	Pilea	*Pilea serpyllacea*
18.	Variegata	*Pedialanthus tithymaloidis*
19.	Marble queen	*Scinapsus aureus*
20.	Nanus	*Pedilanthus tithymoloides*

S. No.	Common Name	Botanical Name
21.	Fern	*Ptris, Dryopteris and Adiantum*
22.	Peepal	*Ficus religiosa*
FLOWERING PLANTS		
23.	English & Indian rose	*Rose alba*
24.	China rose	*Hibiscus rose sinensis*
25.	Glory of garden (Bougainvillea)	*Bougainvillea spectabilis*
26.	Football lilly	*Heamanthus multiflowers*
27.	Gladiolus	*Gladiolus tristus*
28.	Aster	*Aster sp.*
29.	Nusturtium	*Nusturtium sp.*
30.	Pansy	*Viola sp.*
31.	Nine O'Clock	*Portulaca species*
32.	Dahlia	*Dahlia sp.*
33.	Chrysanthemum	*Chrysanthemum cinerariaefoluim*
34.	Marigold	*Tagetes patula*
FRUIT PLANTS		
35.	Gauva	*Psidium quajava*
36.	Banana	*Musa paradisiaca*
37.	Lemon	*Citrus limon*
38.	Strawberry	*Fragaria vesca*
VEGETABLE PLANTS		
39.	Tomato	*Lycopersicon esculentum*
40.	Chilly	*Capsicum annuum*
41.	Boro (Cowpea)	*Vigna sinensis*
42.	French bean	*Phaseolus vulgaris*
43.	Cucumber	*Cucumis sp*
44.	Radish	*Raphanus sativus*
CACTI / SUCCULENT PLANTS		
45.	Sansveria	*Sansveria frifaciata*
46.	Varigata	*Pleomele reflexa*
47.	Nanus	*Padilanthus titymoloides*
48.	Round cactus (green)	*Melocacuts maxonii*
49.	Rod cactus	*Cereus jamacaru*

APPENDIX V

ESSENTIAL PLANT NUTRIENTS

SN	Chemical Name	Symbol	Function
Macronutrients			
1.	Carbon	C	Component of all organic compounds
2.	Oxygen	O	Supplied by air & water
3.	Hydrogen	H	Supplied by air & water
4.	Nitrogen	N	Part of chlorophyll, amino acids, proteins, nucleic acids
5.	Phosphorus	P	Used in photosynthesis and almost all aspects of growth
6.	Potassium	K	Activates enzymes, used in formation of sugar and starch
7.	Calcium	Ca	Used in cell growth and division, part of cell wall
8.	Magnesium	Mg	Part of chlorophyll, activates enzymes
9.	Sulfur	S	Part of amino acids and proteins
Micronutrients			
10.	Boron	B	Affects reproduction
11.	Chlorine	Cl	Aids in root growth
12.	Copper	Cu	Use in chlorophyll, activates enzymes
13.	Iron	Fe	Used in photosynthesis
14.	Manganese	Mn	Part of chlorophyll, activates enzymes
15.	Zinc	Zn	Part of enzymes, used in auxins
16.	Molybdenum	Mo	Used in nitrogen fixation

APPENDIX VI

CONSTITUENTS OF NUTRIENT SOLUTION

ALBERT'S MIXTURE

S. No.	Nutrient chemicals	Weight in grams
1.	Multi-K (Potassium nitrate)	38.00
2.	Refined grade calcium nitrate	952.00
3.	Magnesium sulphate	308.00
4.	EDTA iron	8.00
5.	Zinc sulphate	0.15
6.	Boric acid	0.20
7.	Manganese sulphate	1.15
8.	Copper sulphate	0.10
9.	Mono potassium phosphate	269.00
10.	Potassium sulphate	423.00
11.	Ammonium molybdate	0.03

APPENDIX VII

WATER QUALITY CLASSES FOR HYDROPONICS

Quality parameters	Unit	Water Quality classes		
		Non-hazardous	Slight to Moderate	Severe
pH		--- Normal Range 6.5 - 8.4 ---		
Salinity Ecw	Ds/m	0.00 – 0.8	0.8 – 3.0	>3
Sodlum	me/lit	<3	<3	-
Chloride	me/lit	<3	<3	-
Boron	me/lit	<0.7	0.7-3	>3
Bicarbonates	me/lit	<1.5	1.5-8.5	>8.5

APPENDIX VIII

FREQUENTLY ASKED QUESTIONS OF HYDROPONICS

1. **Is hydroponics a natural method of plant cultivation?**

   Yes, hydroponics is a natural method of plant cultivation. The Oxford Dictionary defines the word 'natural' as 'existing in or by nature, not artificial, innate, inherent, self-sown, uncultivated'. Conventional soil cultivation has been practiced as early as human civilization was known and this mode of plant production is regarded as natural way. With the introduction of hydroponics, critics are quick to point out that this new technology of plant production is most 'un-natural' because plants obtain their nutrient elements from 'artificial' inorganic fertilizer salts rather than from the soil media. However, it should be pointed out that the inorganic fertilizer salts used by the hydroponics growers to feed their plants provide essentially the same type of inorganic nutrient elements as that of the soil. The only 'un-natural' thing about hydroponic plant cultivation is that the hydroponic grower has made a conscious choice of not feeding the plants with 'junk' (e.g. toxic minerals elements, soil borne disease pathogens etc.) which are universally present in the soil media to a larger or a lesser extent. Centuries ago, to use microbial products known as antibiotics to treat a sick person would have been viewed as a most 'un-natural' way of practicing medicine. However, in today's modern medicine treatment, it would be most 'un-natural' and irresponsible for a physician to totally abstain from using antibiotics knowing fully the immense benefit of antibiotics in saving lives. With the world population escalating to new heights and with the limited amount of arable land available for soil cultivation, it is anticipated that novel and high tech farming methods such as hydroponic technology, which allows high density plant cultivation will be seen less and less of 'un-natural' means of plant production.

2. Is hydroponic an effective and efficient method of cultivation ?

Yes, hydroponic is an effective way of growing plants just like soil cultivation. If a plant is grown without soil and with a complete nutrient solution, plants achieved good growth. They key to success of hydroponics is depend on nutrients solution in hydroponics. Hydroponic crops should be raised on a perfect mixture of primary, secondary and micro-nutrients. The formulas for different crops and environments vary, but all have been defined from extensive experience with a wide variety of crops growing in many different environments throughout the world. Problcms may occur where water quality is poor and where environmental extremes of high or low temperature and humidities places stress on crops; however, when a hydroponic facility is properly planned and installed, the resulting crops can be impressive. Data generated in Europe, Israel, Canada, Australia and the United States have defined precise combinations of minerals for a variety of crops. The data is so accurate that required elements are specified in mS (millisiemens) and US (microsiemens), a system of measuring by electrical conductivity and calculating by atomic weight.

3. Are the organic compost and manure added to the soil superior in providing nutrients to the plants than the hydroponic solution ?

No, as mentioned in the answer to the previous question, hydropoincally grown plants require exactly the same type of inorganic elements as the soil-grown plants for growth. In soil cultivation, organic compost and manure are often added to the soil to improve the soil fertility. This organic matter takes time to decompose into inorganic elements and to convert into available form before they can be absorbed by the plants roots. In hydroponic cultivation, inorganic elements in readily available form are fed directly to the plant roots. This explains why hydroponically grown plants are often reported to outperform the soil grown counterparts in terms of yield and growth rate. The organic manure added to the soil can also impart disease to the plants and pose a health hazard to consumers who eat the raw contaminated plant parts.

4. Are hydroponically grown vegetables stacked with chemicals and do they have a chemical taste?

The taste of hydroponically produced vegetable are better than the vegetables grown in open field systems and do not have a chemical taste. Chemical analyses, carried out by the Chemical Process and Biotechnology Department of the Singapore Polytechnic, had conclusively proved that there were no apparent major differences in the chemical contents in the hydroponically grown vegetables and that of their soil grown counterparts. In fact, most of the trace elements (e.g zinc, copper) were actually found to be lower in the hydroponically grown vegetables largely due to a better control of the concentration of these elements in the nutrient solution. This finding is reassuring as consumption of higher levels of these trace elements can pose a health hazard to the consumers. Sensory evaluation tests carried out by the Singapore Polytechnic on 300 tasters conclusively showed that the general public actually preferred the taste of the hydroponically grown vegetables over the soil grown vegetables. These findings of the Singapore Polytechnic were presented in the 1994 International Conference on Agro-technology in the Commonwealth held at the National University of Singapore.

5. It is true that hydroponic plants grow faster than the soil-grown plants?

Generally speaking, hydroponically grown vegetables, fruits and flowers grown about a third faster than the soil-grown plants. This is because most of the essential nutrients are supplied directly to the plant roots in readily available form and also in the balanced quantity. On other hand, hydroponic plants do not have to compete for the limited amount of nutrient elements as they do in soil. This reason that hydroponic plants grow faster than soil grown plants.

6. **Are hydroponically grown vegetables lower in nutritional values?**

   No, hydroponically grown vegetables have superior nutritive value over soil grown vegetables. In terms of mineral content, the nutritional values of hydroponically grown vegetables and soil grown vegetables are essentially the same. However, research studies carried out by Singapore Polytechnic showed that the vitamin C content of hydroponically grown vegetables is significantly higher than that of the soil grown vegetables.

7. **It is true that hydroponic vegetables are relatively free of pesticide's contamination?**

   Hydroponic vegetables are produced under insect-proof netting and so the incidence of insect-pest outbreak is greatly reduced. Moreover, hydroponic vegetables mature faster and can be harvested earlier than soil grown vegetables. This shortened growth cycle effectively impedes any stray insect-pests from developing to full maturity to cause an outbreak. Thus, in a well managed hydroponic farm, it is unnecessary for a hydroponic grower to fumigate his plant produce with potentially harmful pesticides. Chemical analyses carried out by the Singapore Polytechnic on the hydroponic vegetables from Oh Chin Haut Hydroponic Farm in Singapore showed that they were free of pesticides contaminations.

8. **How is hydroponic cultivation compared to conventional agriculture in terms of yield ?**

   As far as yield is concerned, hydroponics is better way of growing plants than the traditional system of plant growing. Hydroponic cultivation give a much more favourable yield than conventional soil culture due to three reasons (i) faster growth rate of hydroponic plants, (ii) hydroponic cultivation permits intensive or high density planting as plant nutrients and water are always readily available in sufficient quantities, (iii) low incidence of pests and disease outbreak.

For example, it has been reported widely by hydroponic tomato growers worldwide that the yields for tomatoes grown by hydroponics is 3 to 4 times higher over conventional systems.

9. If soil grown plants are cheaper than hydroponic produce, why should I bother with hydroponic produce ?

Generally speaking, hydroponic produce is slightly more expensive than soil grown plants. However, the long term health benefit derived from eating pesticide - free hydroponic produce far outweighs any monetary consideration. The existence of poisoning from pesticide residues in plant produce is well documented worldwide. For example, in 1985, watermelons, which had been sprayed with the carbamate insecticide aldicarb, were linked to an outbreak of severe flu-like illness in 1,000 people in Western United States. The symptoms included profuse sweating, nausea, muscle cramps, twitching, comiting, diarrhoea and blurred vision. There is even greater concern over the long-term health problems associated with pesticides exposure which may include cancers, reduction in sperm density, contamination of mothers, milk, birth deformities and spontaneous abortion.

10. Can mosquitoes thrive in hydroponic solution ?

Research carried out by the Chemical Process and Biotechnology Department of Singapore Polytechnic showed that mosquito larvae could thrive in hydroponic solution at EC values (1.5 mS / cm to 3.0 mS / cm) which are commonly used for hydroponic plant production. It is erroneous to claim that the concentration of the nutrient solution used in hydroponic cultivation is osmotically unfavourable for mosquitoes to thrive. Thus, it is important in a static hydroponic water culture (such as a commercial hydroponic kit which does not utilize a motor pump to recirculate the nutrient solution) that all the planting holes are covered up in order to avoid mosquitoes breeding in the nutrient solution. For a recirculating hydroponic system, complete nutrient solution change over is achieved by the motor pump at regular intervals daily. The incidence of mosquitoes breeding in a fast flowing recirculating system is reduced to almost none. It is also unlikely that the mosquito larvae will survive their journey through the siphoning action of the motor pump.

11. Can all plants be grown hydroponically? What about mushrooms?

Yes, all plants can be grown hydroponically, although some plants perform better in some hydroponic system than others. You can grow all kind of herbs, flowers, vegetables and house plants in hydroponic gardens.

Mushrooms are fungi and they have a completely different mode of nutrition compared to plants. Mushrooms, therefore, cannot be raised successfully with hydroponic nutrient solution alone.

12. Are hydroponically grown vegetables as visually attractive as their soil grown counterparts?

Visual evaluation test carried out at the Chemical Process and Biotechnology Department of Singapore Polytechnic unanimously showed that consumers preferred the clean and healthy appearance of hydroponically grown vegetables as they were free from soil contaminants and insect bite holes.

13. Is hydroponically produced food organic in nature?

There is a huge popular debate about the value of "Organic" fertilizers and methods, many people would like to apply "Organics" to hydroponics. Currently accepted organic fertilizer components are dependent upon organisms in the soil to convert the "Organic" materials into a usable form for plants.

In hydroponics, we provide the minerals required for plant growth directly, completely eliminating the need for soil and soil organisms. The result is much higher growth rates, yields and even crop quality than organic methods can achieve. This is not what some people want to hear, but it is the simple scientific truth and practically all scientists and educators in the fields of agriculture and chemistry know it and will be the first to agree. In fact, the kinds of materials which are permitted for use under "Organic" regulations are not of sufficient purity to be used for hydroponic culture.

We use only the most refined and pure ingredients to blend out hydroponic fertilizers, including food and pharmaceutical materials. "Organic" regulations do not permit purified or refined ingredients to be used, all "organic" fertilizer ingredients must be in their natural, unrefined form – the result can be detrimental levels of impurities and toxins plus very poor solubility. "Organic" is a matter of bureaucratic definitions, not science. Organic is a method of farming, not a definition of the produce itself. There's no such thing as "organic produce", there's only "organically grown produce."

With this in mind it is important to recognize the reasons that "organically" grown produce is gaining such popularity. Consumers want to buy produce which is not tainted with hazardous chemicals or poisons. There is an increasing public demand for methods which are gentle on out delicate planet and which don't harm the soil, water or ecosystems. Hydroponic farming methods fit properly into this system of values if used appropriately. Hydroponics protects soil because it does not use soil. Less water is required for hydroponic culture and consequently more food can be cultivated with less water. The fertilizers we use for hydroponics are ultra-pure and leave not residue in the cultivated fruits and vegetables. Since hydroponic technologies are more efficient that soil methods, more people can be fed with less area and ecological impact.

14. Can I earn some money from hydroponics?

The successful stories of many hydroponic companies and commercial hydroponic growers in many parts of the world published in hydroponic magazines and journals augur well for the future of hydroponic industry. As a general rule, a commercial hydroponic grower may be limited in growing crops that give a rapid turnover such as vegetables in his earlier years of operation to cover the high capital cost of investment. Many hydroponic companies which specialize in marketing hydroponic kits, nutrient formulations and hydroponic growth media, have also made it big on the international scene.

15. Will hydroponic technology be obsolete in another fifty years or so?

No, Hydroponic technology is widely recognized as a practical answer to meet the increasing demand for food in countries that lack arable land. As food and land shortages will undoubtedly increase in fifty years from now, hydroponic technology should play even more significant role then.

16. Do I need a sound knowledge of chemistry to practice hydroponics ?

Many hydroponic companies provide a wide range of ready mixed nutrient formulations that will meet the needs of any amateur growers who know very little chemistry. However, since hydroponics is a specialized form of horticulture, for a commercial hydroponic growers to have a basic understanding of chemistry of nutrient formulations as different crops may have different nutritional requirements for optimal growth. Besides this, a commercial grower also needs to have a working knowledge of plant physiology and plant pathology to handle the many horticultural problems encountered in his routine operations.

17. What are the advantages of hydroponics over soil?

Plants grown in hydroponic systems maintain optimum nutrient and moisture levels, so they grow faster and healthier. In hydroponics, no soil means no weeds and no soil-born pests or diseases. Another advantage is that root systems stay smaller on hydroponically grown plants, allowing the plant to focus its growth energy on producing plant mass rather than roots. This means you can have more plants per square foot of growing space. And since hydroponic plants never get root bound, they don't need to be repotted. Hydroponic produce has a longer shelf life than soil grown produce.

GLOSSARY

Absorption: Uptake of nutrients from the soil by plant roots, or directly into the leaves from foliar sprays.

Adsorption: The attachment of nutrient ions to the surface of clay and organic colloids within the soil.

Aeration: Supplying soil and roots with air or oxygen.

Alkaline: Refers to soil or solution with a high pH. Any pH over 7 is considered alkaline.

Aero-Hydroponics: A method which uses rockwool, net pots, vine clips or other devices to support the plant while its roots grow in the air under a constant mist of nutrient solution.

Aeroponics: A method which uses rockwool, net pots, vine clips or other devices to support the plant while its roots grow completely submerged in nutrient solution.

Aggregate culture: A system in which a material such as sand, gravel or marbles supports the plant roots.

Algal bloom: Excessive algal growth caused by an oversupply of nutrients in a waterway.

Ammonification A process by which some soil organisms, 'ammonifiers', convert soil organic nitrogen to ammonium ions.

Anion exchange capacity A measure of the soil's ability to hold negatively-charged nutrient ions for plant use.

Aqua culture: A system in which the plant roots are immensed in water containing dissolved nutrients.

Aquaponics: the integration of aquaculture (the raising of marine animals, such as fish) with hydroponics; the waste products from the fish are treated and then used to fertilize hydroponically growing plants.

Auxin: A kind of plant hormones which is responsible for foliage and root elongation.

Ballast: The electrical components (usually a transformer and capacitor) that energize a high intensity bulb.

Beneficiation A process of removing clay and other impurities from phosphate rock to upgrade the phosphorus content of the rock.

Biodegradable: Able to decompose or breakdown through natural bacterial action: Substances made of organic matter are biodegradable.

Bloom Booster, Blossom Booster: Fertilizer having high amount of phosphorus (P) that increases flower yield.

Bolt: term used to describe a plant that has gone to seed prematurely.

Bolting: for a plant to prematurely begin the development of a flowering stalk and, subsequently, seed.

Bonsai: a very short or dwarfed plant.

Branch tips: roots seldom grow beyond the drip line.

Breaker box: electrical circuit box having on / off switches rather than fuses.

Breathe: roots draw in or breathe oxygen, stomata draw in or breathe carbon dioxide.

Bud blight: a withering condition that attacks flower buds.

Buffering: The ability of a substance to reduce shock and cushion against pH fluctuations.

Bulb: the outer glass envelope or jacket that protects the arc tube of an hid lamp.

Burn: Leaf tips that turn dark from excess fertilizer and salt burn.

Capillary action: when the surface of a liquid is in contact with a solid, the liquid is elevated or depressed depending upon the relative attraction of the molecules of the liquid for each other or for those of the solid. This is similar to how plants seemingly defy gravity when they transport liquid from the roots upward through the plant.

Cation exchange capacity A measure of the soil's ability to hold positively-charged nutrient ions for plant use.

Caustic: capable of destroying, killing or eating away by chemical activity.

Cfm: cubic feet per minute.

Chelate: combining nutrients in an atomic ring that is easy for plants to absorb.

Chlorophyll: the green material in plants that is created in the presence of light and is instrumental in photosynthesis.

Chlorosis: The condition of a sick plant with yellowing leaves due to inadequate formation of chlorophyll. Chlorosis is caused by a nutrient deficiency, usually iron or nitrogen; nutrient deficiencies are themselves often caused by a pH that is out of the acceptable range.

Clay: soil made of very fine organic mineral particles, clay is not suitable for container gardening.

Color spectrum: the band of colors (measured in nm) emitted by a light source.

Color tracer: a coloring agent added to many commercial fertilizers, so the horticulturist knows there is fertilizer in the solution.

Cladosporium: any of several fungal diseases that afflict plants; commonly called leaf mold.

Clone: A plant produced through asexual reproduction including, but not limited to, cuttings, layering and tissue culture.

Closed system: a hydroponic system, like nutrient film technique (NFT) systems, that recirculates the nutrient solution.

Coconut Fiber Coir: Not used much in the United States, but due to the low cost it is used in tropical countries. Not recommended for recirculating systems due to leaching of organics into the water.

Color Temperature: A measure of color of light emitted by a bulb in comparison to black (also known as Kelvin temperature or correlated color temperature). This is used as a general measure of a bulb's coolness (whiter light) or warmness (redder light).

Compaction: soil condition that results from tightly packing soil; compacted soil allows for only marginal aeration and root penetration.

Companion planting: planting garlic, marigolds, etc., along with other plants to discourage insect infestation.

Conditioning: To soak new Rockwool in an acidic solution to lower the pH from 8.0 to 5.5.

Conductivity: the scale, described as electrical conductivity (EC) or conductivity factor (CF), that is used to measure the strength of nutrient solution. Pure water does not conduct electricity. But as salts are dissolved into the pure water, electricity begins to be conducted. An electrical current will begin to flow when live electrodes are placed into the solution. The more salts that are dissolved, the stronger the salt solution and, correspondingly, the more electrical current that will flow. This current flow is connected to special electronic circuitry that allows the grower to determine the resultant strength of the nutrient solution.

Continuous flow systems – A system in which the nutrient solution flows constantly over the plant roots. This system is the one most commonly used for commercial production.

Controlled environmental agriculture: It is a system of plant growing in which environmental parameters i.e. light, temperature, water, oxygen, carbon dioxide, pH and nutrients are kept under complete control.

Core: the transformer in the ballast is referred to as the core in hid lighting systems.

Corms, rhizomes and tubers: dormant terms planted in the fall for spring blooms, or forced indoors for winter blooms. Common varieties are dahlias and irises.

Cross-pollination: transferring pollen from the flowers of one plant of a species to the stigma of another plant of the same species.

Crushed granite: In hydroponics, screened crushed granite of approximate particle size of 2 mm should be used. The medium is totally inert, but has a relatively low water retention capacity. The medium can be reused over a period of time.

Cutting: (1) growing tip cut from a parent plant for asexual propagation (2) clone.

C:N ratio: The ratio of organic carbon to total nitrogen in a soil. Provides a measure of the quality and rate of decomposition of organic matter. The lower the ratio, the quicker organic matter will break down, and release nutrients (including nitrogen) in available form for plant uptake.

Damping-off: Disease caused by fungus i.e, phythium species that attacks young seedlings and cuttings, causing stems to rot at the base; over watering is the main cause of damping-off.

Deficiency Visual symptoms of a nutrient disorder which appears when a plant's uptake is in-sufficient.

Denitrification: A process by which some soil organisms convert nitrate to nitrous oxides and nitrogen gas which are then lost to the atmosphere. Occurs particularly in waterlogged soils, i.e. under anaerobic conditions.

Direct current (dc): an electric current that flows in only one direction.

Deplete: exhaust soil of nutrients, making it infertile. Desiccate: cause to dry up.

Dioecious: varieties or species with male and female flowers on separate plants.

Dissolved Solids: The amount of dissolved solids, usually fertilizer salts, that are measured in water in parts per million.

Dome: the part of the hid outer bulb opposite the neck and threads.

Dome support: the spring like brackets that mount the arc tube within the outer envelope.

Drainage: A way to empty soil of excess water: with good drainage, water passes through soil evenly.

Drip Aeration: A hydroponic method wherein air pressure from a small air pump is used to percolate nutrient solution out through a ring of feeder tubing which encircles the plant.

Drip line: a line around a plant directly under its outermost.

Drip Method: A very efficient watering system that employs a main hole with small water emitters. Water is metered out of the emitters, one drop at a time. The most popular among commercial applications: leaching of salt build up, smaller reservoirs, and less nutrients are just a few of the positive traits of a drip system.

Dry ice: a cold, white substance formed when carbon dioxide is compressed and cooled; dry ice changes into CO_2 gas at room temperature.

Ebb & Flow: A hydroponic system in which the medium, usually aggregate pebbles, is periodically flooded with nutrient solution and then drained again, feeding and aerating the medium and root system.

Elongate: grow in length.

Equinox: the point at which the sun crosses the equator and day and night are each 12 hours long; the equinox occurs twice a year, in spring and fall.

Eutrophication An overgrowth of weeds or algae in a waterway due to an excess of nutrients in a waterway. This may initially support higher fish populations, but the death and decay of water plants can deplete the water of oxygen, resulting in fish kills.

Feed: deliver nutrient to the plant via roots or foliage.

Fertigate: to fertilize and irrigate at the same time.

Fluorescent lamp: electric lamp using a tube filled with fluorescent material, which has a low heat output.

Fertilizer Burn: Over fertilization: First leaf tips burn (turn yellow or brown) then the leaves curl.

Fertilizer Any natural or manufactured material added to soil to supply an essential plant nutrient.

Fired Clay Pebbles: This is a high performance growing media. The clay pebbles are either formed from clay and fired, or milled form shale rock, and then fired. In either case the end result is a porous interior surrounded by a less porous hard shell. The less porous hard shell prevents the media from degrading in the presence of water. The capillary action is very high. Three sizes are available.

Fixation Process by which available plant nutrients become unavailable by reaction with components of the soil. Phosphorus and potassium may both undergo fixation, leading to decreased availability in the soil.

Foliar Feeding: Misting plants with fertilizer solution which is absorbed by the foliage.

Footcandle: A unit of illumination equal to the intensity of one candle at a distance of one foot. Footcandles are usually used as a measure of light received.

Fungus: A lower plant lacking chlorophyll which may attack green plants: Mold, rust, mildew, mushrooms and bacteria are fungi. Common fungal diseases that attack plants are "damping-off," Botrytis, and powdery mildew.

Fungistat: a product that inhibits fungus keeping it in check.

Fusarium: any of several fungal diseases that afflict plants; commonly called dry rot or wilt.

Fuse box: box containing fuses that control electric circuits.

Geolite: One of several brand names/varieties of clay aggregate medium (also known as LECA for light expanded clay aggregate). It is a lightweight, porous substrate with excellent aeration. Because it does not really wick water effectively, Geolite and other LECA mediums are favorites in ebb-and-flow and drip hydroponic systems.

Genetic make up: the set of genes inherited from parent plants.

Germination: the activation of a seed causing it to start to grow; also the production of a pollen tube by a pollen grain.

Gravel Culture: Roots of plants growing in a solid aggregate composed of particles with a diameter more than 3 mm. Gravel, basalt, scoria, pumice, plastic, and other inorganic material. The size of most gravel used is between 5 to 10 mm in diameter, with rounded edges preferred.

Growing medium: materials that are sometimes used in hydroponic growing to support the plant's roots and, sometimes, to hold nutrient.

Gypsum: Hydrated calcium sulfate ($CaSO_4.2H_2O$), mainly used as a soil conditioner. Either mined from natural sources or produced as a by-product of the manufacture of phosphoric acid, the latter being known as phosphogypsum.

Gpm: gallons per minute.

Harden-off: To gradually acclimatize a plant to a more harsh environment. A seedling must be hardened-off before planting outdoors.

Hermaphrodite: A plant having both male and female organs; the breeding of hermaphrodites is hard to control.

Hertz (hz): a unit if a frequency that cycles one time each second: a home with 60 hertz ac current cycles 60 times per second.

H.I.D. (High Intensity Discharge) Lights: Metal Halide (MH) and High Pressure Sodium (HPS) lamps belong to the HID family of lights. They are used for garden lighting because of their high light output per watt, and the spectral distribution of their light.

Hood: reflective cover of a hid lamp.

Hor: the abbreviation stamped on some hid bulbs meaning they must be burned in a horizontal position.

Horticultural Rockwool Culture: Roots of plants growing in horticultural rockwool or any similar material. This method really came into its own during the 1980s, after research in the 1970s.

Hormone: Chemical substance that controls the growth and development of a plant. Root-inducing hormones help cuttings root.

Humidity (Relative): Ratio between the amount of moisture in the air and the greatest amount of moisture the air could hold at the same temperature.

Humus: Fraction of soil organic matter which remains after plant and animal residues have decomposed.

Hybrid: The offspring from two plants of different breeds, variety or genetic make-up.

Hydrated Lime: Instantly soluble lime, used to raise or lower pH.

Hygrometer: Instrument for measuring relative humidity in the atmosphere: A hygrometer will save time, frustration and money.

Hydroculture: All systems or methods of hydroponics, if used especially for growing ornamentals in the home or office. It usually means using fired clay pebbles in a passive system with no pump. Excellent for slow growing house plants like ferns or orchids.

Hydroponics: The science of growing plants in water. Where the plant's roots are grown in an inorganic medium and the water holds all the nutrients.

Immobilisation: Process whereby nutrients in inorganic form are converted to organic form by incorporation into micro-organisms. These nutrients are then temporarily unavailable for plant uptake.

Inert: chemically non-reactive; inert growing mediums make it easy to control the chemistry of the nutrient solution.

Intensity: the magnitude of the light energy per unit; intensity diminishes the farther away from the source.

Kilowatt hour: measure of electricity used per hour; a 1000-watt hid uses one kilowatt in one hour.

Labile Meaning 'inclined to change', it describes a soil nutrient which may become available for plant uptake.

Lacewing: beneficial insects that preys on aphids.

Leach: Dissolve or wash out soluble components of soil by heavy watering.

Leaching: Deep percolation or washing of nutrients through the soil to a depth beyond the root zone of plants.

Leaf Curl: Leaf malformation due to over watering, over fertilization, lack of magnesium, insect or fungus damage or negative tropism.

L.E.C.A (Light Expanded Clay Aggregate): is a grow medium formed from natural clay baked into pellets.

Leggy: Abnormally tall, with sparse foliage: Leggyness of a plant is usually caused by lack of light.

Life cycle: a series of growth stages through which a plant must pass in its natural lifetime; the stages for an annual plant are seed, seedling, vegetative and floral.

Light Mover: A device that moves a lamp back and forth across the ceiling of a garden room to provide more even distribution of light.

Lime A calcium based material used to raise the pH of acidic soils. Refers mainly to calcium carbonate.

Litmus paper: chemically sensitive paper used for testing pH.

Loam: organic soil mixture of crumbly clay, silt and sand.

Lumen: A unit of illumination; a measurement of light output. One lumen is equal to the light emitted by one candle that falls on one square foot of surface located one foot away from the candle.

Macronutrients: the major minerals that are used by plants in large amounts, consisting of nitrogen (N), phosphorus (P), potassium (K), sulphur (S), calcium (Ca), and magnesium (Mg).

Manganese (Mn): This micronutrient activates one or more enzymes in fatty acid synthesis; it also activates the enzymes responsible for DNA and RNA production. Closely associated with copper and zinc, manganese also participates directly in the photosynthetic creation of oxygen from water.

Mean: average throughout life; hid's are rated in mean lumens.

Medium: The substrate or soilless material which supports the plant and absorbs and releases the nutrient solution in hydroponic horticulture.

Meristem: tip of plants growth.

Micronutrients: the minor minerals that are used by plants in small amounts, consisting of boron (B), copper (Cu), cobalt (Co), iron (Fe), manganese (Mn), molybdenum (Mo), and zinc (Zn).

Mineral deficiency: when a plant is not receiving a required nutrient--at all or in an insufficient amount--a disorder will result.

Mineralization: Process carried out by soil micro-organisms whereby nutrients are released in an inorganic form from the decomposition of organic matter.

Mixes: A 50/50 mix of perlite/vermiculite makes an ideal growing medium. It is advisable not to mix sand, scoria or crushed granite with Perlite or vermiculite, as they will separate when wet due to differences in densities.

Mobile nutrients: Those nutrients which move freely with soil moisture, or can be moved within the plant from older tissues to younger tissues. Some nutrients can be immobile in soils, and mobile in plants, and vice versa.

Moisture meter: an electronic device that measures the exact moisture content of soil at any given point.

Monochromatic: producing only one color; lp sodium lamps are monochromatic.

Monoecious: varieties or species with separate male and female flowers on each plant.

Mulching: Spreading of material e.g. plant litter or plastic on the surface of soil to protect the soil from erosion or to control weeds. Organic mulches can also improve the soil's organic matter content and tilth.

Nanometer: 0.000001 meters, nm is used as a scale to measure wave lengths of light; color and light spectrums are expressed in nanometers (nm).

Necrosis: The dying of plant tissue, usually the result of serious nutrient deficiency or pest attack.

Nitrogen (N): Nitrogen is used in various forms to promote rapid vegetative growth, leaf, flower, fruit and seed development, and chlorophyll development; and to increase the protein content in all plants.

Nitrification: A process by which soil organisms, 'nitrifiers', use oxygen to convert ammonium ions to nitrate ions.

Nitrogen fixation: The conversion of molecular nitrogen (N_2) into nitrogen compounds suitable for plant uptake. This process is carried out by certain micro-organisms, such as Rhizobium bacteria in the nodules on the roots of legumes. This is of immediate benefit to the host plant.

Non-labile: Describes a soil nutrient which is tied up in the soil and therefore unavailable for plant uptake.

Nutrient Film Technique: NFT is the method of using shallow troughs with lids where a thin nutrient solution film streams along the bottom of the channels. Ideal for lettuce, herbs, strawberries and flowers.

Nutrient Solution: minerals dissolved in water that are used to feed hydroponically grown plants.

Nutrients: The elements needed by plants for normal growth and health. The major nutrients (MACRONUTRIENTS) are nitrogen (N), phosphorus (P), and potassium (K), but there are numerous MICRONUTRIENTS (also called TRACE ELEMENTS) which also have integral roles in maintaining plant health. A good quality hydroponic nutrient formula will contain all of the major nutrients and micronutrients needed by the vast majority of plants.

Nutrients, Secondary: The elements other than N, P and K which are considered nearly as important as N, P and K but are not considered micronutrients. Calcium (Ca), magnesium (Mg), and sulphur (S) are the elements usually referred to by this term.

Ohm's power law: a law that expresses the strength of an electric current; volts times amperes equals watts.

Organic: made of, or derived from or related to living organisms. In agriculture organic means "natural". In chemistry organic means "a molecule or substance that contains carbon".

Osmosis: the flow or diffusion that takes place through a semi-permeable membrane typically separating a solvent and a solution that strives to bring about a condition of equilibrium.

Ovule: a plant's egg found within the calyx, it contains all the female genes; when fertilized, an ovule will grow into a seed.

Parasite: organism that lives on or in another host organism; fungus is a parasite.

Parts per million (ppm): a ratio figure that represents the amount of one substance that is in one million parts of another substance; commonly used to describe the relative concentrations of nutrient solutions.

Passive: A hydroponic system without a pump. The plants take up nutrients through a fibrous wick from the pot to the nutrient solution. The solution will generally have a bubbler to maintain proper oxygenation.

Peat: partially decomposed vegetation (usually moss) with slow decay due to extreme moisture and cold.

Perlite: Sand or volcanic glass which has been expanded by heat; perlite holds water and nutrients on its many irregular surfaces.

pH: a measurement of a nutrient solution's relative concentration of positive hydrogen ions: a pH of 7 is considered neutral; below 7 is called acidic; above 7 is called alkaline.

pH tester: electronic instrument or chemical used to find where soil or water is on the ph scale.

Photometrics: the study of light, especially color.

Phosphor coating: internal bulb coating that diffuses light and is responsible for variations in color outputs.

Phototropism: the specific movement of a plant part towards a light source.

Photoperiod: The relative hours of light and darkness in a 24-hour period. Some plants respond to a change in day length (photoperiod) in order to grow or flower.

Photosynthesis: the formation of carbohydrates from carbon dioxide (CO_2) and a source of hydrogen (H)--such as water--in chlorophyll-containing cells exposed to light involving a photochemical release of oxygen through the decomposition of water.

Pigment: the substance in paint or anything that absorbs light, producing (reflecting) the same color.

Pistil: the entire female section of the flower, including the eggs, ovary, style, and stigma.

Pollen: the mass of microspores in a seed plant that usually appears as a fine dust and is the agent of pollination.

Pollination: the transfer of pollen from the male part of a flower (stamen) to the female part of a flower (the style and stigma).

Power surge: interruption or change in intensity of electricity.

Primary Nutrients: N (nitrogen), P (phosphorus), K (potassium).

Propagate: 1. Sexual-produce a seed by breeding different male and female flowers 2. Asexual-to produce a plant by taking cuttings.

Prune: alter the shape and growth pattern of a plant by cutting stems and shoots.

PVC pipe: plastic (polyvinyl chloride) pipe that is easy to work with, readily available and used to pipe water into a garden room.

Pyrethrum: Natural insecticide made from the blossoms of various chrysanthemums. Pyrethrum is the most effective natural spider mite exterminator.

Rejuvenate: restore youth; a mature plant, having completed its life cycle (flowering), may be stimulated by a new 18 hour photoperiod, to rejuvenate or produce new vegetative growth.

Reservoir: The container in a hydroponic system which holds nutrient solution in reserve for use.

Reverse Osmosis: the process of removing minerals from water, which is forced by pressure through a differentially permeable membrane, filtering out the minerals; can happen when growers accidentally apply too strong of a nutrient to a plant's roots, leeching life out of the plant.

Rhizobiurn bacteria Nitrogen fixing bacteria found in the root nodules of leguminous plants.

Rockwool: Inert, soilless growing medium consisting of woven, thin strand-like fibers made from molten volcanic rock and limestone, which is heated to over 2900 degrees F, extruded, and formed into slabs, cubes and blocks.

Root bound: bound, stifled or inhibited from normal growth, by the confines of a container; root system becomes pot bound.

Sand Culture: Roots of plants growing in a solid aggregate of particles with a diameter less than 3 mm. Fine perlite, plastic beads, and washed river sand have all been used. Beach sand is too fine, giving inadequate aeration of the roots.

Sand: Coarse washed river sand is a mixture of fine and coarse particles. Sand in the 0.5 mm to 2.5 mm range is most suitable, allowing drainage and good aeration. Between 20-25 per cent by volume of peat moss may be added to improve moisture retention. Builder's sand may be used as long as it does not contain large quantities of fine broken shell which will increase the alkalinity of the medium.

Saline soil: Soil in which plant growth is affected by high levels of salinity, normally associated with sodium chloride.

Salt: crystalline compound that results from improper pH or toxic buildup of fertilizer. Salt will burn plants, preventing them from absorbing nutrients.

Salt index: A measure of the ratio of change in osmotic pressure caused by different fertilizers. Fertilizers with high salt index may cause damage when applied near or in direct contact with seeds.

Scoria: Scoria is a relatively porous volcanic rock which is very good as a medium. Generally a mixture of fine and coarse scoria is used, being heavy enough to support plants yet having good aeration. It is sold as lava rock in many hardware stores.

Secondary Nutrients: Calcium (Ca), magnesium (Mg) and Sulphur (S) which are of secondary importance

Short circuit: condition that results when wires cross and form a circuit. A short circuit will blow fuses.

Shredded Fir Bark (or coarse fir sawdust): Again, low in cost but not recommended for recirculating systems due to the leaching of large amounts of tannic acid into the water. Canadian tomato growers used to use non-recirculating drip systems with coarse sawdust with good results. The sawdust must be replaced each season. Orchid growers use fir bark, as it simulates the natural way they grow on trees, and does not hold excess water.

Side-dressed: Application of fertilizer to the side of crop rows after the seedlings have emerged.

Socket: threaded, wired receptacle for a bulb.

Sodic soil: Soil in which the structure has been affected by high concentrations of exchangeable sodium.

Soil fertility: The status of soil with respect to the amount and availability of essential nutrients.

Soluble: able to be dissolved in water.

Split application: Splitting the seasonal fertilizer requirement for an annual crop, or that required over a year for a perennial crop, into a number of smaller applications. Commonly used for nitrogen and potassium, which are subject to loss through leaching and in other ways.

Sprout: (1) a recently germinated seed (2) small new growth of a leaf or stem.

Stalk: on a male flower, the portion of the stamen that supports the anther.

Stamen: the basic part of the male flower that includes the stalk (or filament), anther, and pollen.

Sterilize: make sterile (super clean) by removing dirt, germs and bacteria.

Sterilization: the act of rendering something free from living cells. In hydroponics it is essential that all materials (especially any growing medium) used are sterile to avoid contaminating the hydroponic system. Steam and chemical agents are often used in this process.

Stigma: the surface at the end of the pistil on a female flower where pollen lands and germinates.

Stroboscopic effect: a quick pulsating or flashing of a lamp.

Stress: a physical or chemical factor that causes extra exertion by plants; a stressed plant will not grow as well as a non stressed plant.

Sugar: food product of plant. Carbohydrates that contain hydrocarbon chain

Style: the part of a female flower that supports the stigma.

Systemic: Used in reference to a disease within the plant tissue, not initiated from the external cells. Also refers to materials and compounds which are taken up or absorbed by the plant and designed to fight disease (e.g. systemic fungicide).

Synthesis: production of a substance, such as chlorophyll, by uniting light energy and elements or chemical compounds.

Tap root: the main or primary root that grows from the seed; lateral roots will branch off the tap root.

Tepid: warm 70 to 80 degrees F (21 to 27 degrees C); always use tepid water around plants to facilitate chemical processes and ease shock.

Terminal bud: bud at the growing end of the main stem.

Thin: cull or weed out weak, slow growing seedlings.

Transformer: a devise in the ballast that transforms electric power from one voltage to another.

Transpire: give off water vapor and by products via stomata and carbon dioxide intake at the leaves.

Trellis: Frame of small boards (lattice) that trains or supports plants.

Top-dressed Uniform broadcast application of fertilizer to the soil surface after a crop or pasture has become established.

Tungsten: a heavy, hard metal with high melting point which conducts electricity well; tungsten is used for a filament in tungsten halogen and incandescent lamps.

Ultraviolet: light with very short wave lengths, out of the visible spectrum, past the blue-violet.

VAM (Vesicular Arbuscular Mycorrhiza): a type of soil fungus infecting the roots of some plants and assisting in the uptake of phosphorus and other immobile soil nutrients.

Vent: opening such as a window or door that allows the circulation of fresh air.

Vermiculite: An expended mica which has been processed and expanded by heat. Vermiculite has excellent water-retention qualities and is a good soil amendment and medium for rooting cuttings. Because of its flaky structure, vermiculite eventually breaks down and requires replacement every 2-4 years. Works well in warm climates.

Vertical: up and down perpendicular to the horizontal. Wetting agent: compound that reduces the droplet size and lowers the surface tension of the water, making it wetter.

Vermiculaponics: Roots of plants growing in vermiculite, or a mixture of vermiculite with any other organic material. This works very well for small experimental systems.

Verticillium: any of several fungal diseases that afflict plants; commonly called wilt.

Volatilisation Process by which certain soluble soil nutrients are changed from solid or aqueous forms to gaseous forms and are lost from the soil to the atmosphere e.g. ammonium (NH,') to ammonia gas (NH_3).

Water Culture: Roots of plants submerged in the nutrient solution with little or no growing media. The Nutrient Film Technique (NFT) is an example.

Wick: woven fiber used in some hydroponic systems to draw nutrient to a plant's roots through capillary action.

REFERENCES

Bauerle, W. L. 1984. Bag culture productivity of green house tomatoes. Special Circular 108. Columbus: Ohio State Univ.

Boodley, J. W., and R. Sheldrakejr, 1977. Cornell peatlite mixes for commercial plant growing. Informational Bulletin 43. New York State College of Agriculture and Life Sciences.

Brad, G. and W. Wiebe, 1997. Tomato Diseases: A Practical Guide for Seedsmen, Growers, and Agricultural Advisors. Seminis Vegetable Seeds, Inc. Saticoy, California, USA.

Cooper, A. J. 1979. *The ABC of NFT.* London: Grower Books.

Cooper, Allen, 1988. *The ABC of NFT*. Grower Books, London.

Douglas, H. M. 1993. Greenhouse Crops in North America: A Practical Guide to Stonewool Culture. Grodania A/S, Canada.

Douglas, James Sholto, 1976. *Advanced Guide to Hydroponics*. Pelham Books. London.

FAO. Soilless Culture for Horticultural Crop Production. FAO Plant Production and Protection Paper 101. 1990.

Fontes, M. R. 1973. Controlled-environment horticulture in the Arabian Desert at Abu Dhabi. *Hort. Sci., 8*:13-16.

Gericke, W. F. 1940. The complete guide to soilless gardening. Prentice-Hall. Englewood Cliffs. N. J.

Graves, C. G. 1983. The nutrient film technique. *Hort. Rev., 5*: l-44.

Growing Edge magazine http://growingedge. com/basics/tutorial/

Hoagland, D. R. and D. I. Arnon, 1938. The water culture method for growing plants without soil. California. Agr. Expt. Sta. Circ. 347.

Howard, M. R. 1995. Hydroponic Food Production, A Definitive Guidebook of Soilless Food-Growing Methods. 5th Ed. Woodbridge Press Publishing Company, Santa Barbara, California, USA.

Ikeda, Hideo, 1984. Recent development of hydroponics in Japan. In: *Proceedings of Sixth International Congress on Soilless Culture*, Lunteren, pp. 661-672.

Ikeda, Hideo, 1985. Soilless culture in Japan. *Farming Japan* 19, 6: 36-42.

Jensen, M. H. and M. A. Teran, 1971. Use of controlled environment for vegetable production in desert regions of the world. *Hort Sci.*, 6:33-36.

Jensen, M. H. and W. L. Collins, 1985. Hydroponic vegetable production. *Hort. Rev.* 7:483-558.

Johnson, H. 1980. Hydroponics: A guide to soilless culture. Leaflet 2947. Berkeley: Division of Agriculture and Natural Resources, Univ. of California.

Kao, Te-Chen, S. T. Chang, T. S. Hong and C. L. Liang, 1989. A novel system design for tropical hydroponic techniques — An improvement on the DRF hydroponic system. *The Second Proceedings of a Symposium on Horticultural Production under Structures*. Taichung, ROC on Taiwan, pp. 130-147. (In Chinese).

Kao, Te-Chen, 1987. Evaluation of the DRF hydroponic vegetable culture system. In: *The First Proceedings of a Symposium on Horticultural Production under Structures.* Taichung, ROC on Taiwan. (In Chinese)

Kao, Te-Chen, 1988. The efficiency of DRF hydroponic system in tropical areas — A comparison with Shinwa Equivalent Exchange System. Paper delivered at an International Symposium on High Technology in Protected Cultivation, held in Hamamatsu, Japan.

Kao, Te-Chen, 1990. Development of a hydroponic vegetable system. In: *Proceedings of the 1990 Chinese American Academic and Professional Convention*. New York, USA.

Kuo, Fu-Yao, 1987. The study and outlook of the facility cultivation on the production of vegetable in Taiwan pp. 31-42. In: *The First Proceedings of a Symposium on Horticultural Production under Structures*, held in Taichung, ROC on Taiwan. pp. 31-42. (In Chinese)

Lorenz., O. A. and K. B. Tyler, 1983. Plant tissue analysis of vegetable crops. In Soil and Plant Testing in California. Bulletin: 1879. Berkeley: Division of Agriculture and Natural Resources, Univ. of California.

Manning, R. 1880. Eds. History of the Massachusetts Horticultural Society 1829-1878. Mass. Hort. Soc., Boston.

Merle H. J. and A. J. Malter, 1995. Hydroponic Nutrients - Easy Ways to Make Your Own, 3rd Ed. by: M Edward Muckle. Protected Agriculture, A Global Review. World Bank Technical Paper Number 253. World Bank, Washington, DC, USA.

Nordstrom, D. K., C. N. Alpers, C. J. Ptacek, D. W. Blowes, 2000. Negative pH and Extremely Acidic Mine Waters from Iron Mountain, California. *Environmental Science.*

Resh, Howard M. 1987. *Hydroponic Food Production.* Woodbridge Press Publishing Company.

Runia, W. T. 1995. A review of possibilities for disinfection of recirculation water from soilless cultures. Glasshouse Crops Res. Sta., Naaldwijk, Holland. p. 9.

Sheldrake, R., S. L. Dallwyn, and D. M. Sangster, 1971. Slow-release fertilizer for greenhouse tomatoes. *New York's Food and Life Sciences 4(2/* 3):10-11.

Shive, J. W. and W. R. Robbins, 1937. Methods of growing plants in solution and sand cultures. New Jersey Agr. Expt. Sta. Bul. 636.

Suzuki, Y., Shinohara, Y., Shibuya, M. and Ikeda, H. 1984. Recent development of Hydroponics in Japan. In: *Proceedings of the International Congress on Soilless Culture*, Lunteren, pp. 661-762.

TAPMC. 1988. *Market Yearbook 1987*. Taiwan Agricultural Products Marketing Corporation, Taipei, ROC on Taiwan.

Virginia Hydroponics, Inc. http://www. hydro4u. com/resource_centre/

Ward, G. M. 1973. Leaf analysis of vegetable crops. Agdex 290/5 32. Ontario, Canada: Ontario Ministry of Agriculture.

Withrow, R. B. and A. P. Withrow, 1948. Nutriculture. S. C. 328. Purdue Univ. Agr. Expt Sta. W. Lafayette, Md.

Witmer, S. H., and S. Honma, 1979. Greenhouse tomatoes, lettuce, and cucumbers. East Lansing: Michigan State Univ. Press.

SUBJECT INDEX

Acidity constant, 91
Aeroponics, 41, 42
Aggregate systems, 37
Albert's mixture, 154
Allium tuberosum Rottl, Ex. K., 50
Amaranthus tricolor L., 50
Apium, graveolens L., 50
Artificial lighting, 120
Balancing elements, 77
Bioplantomin, 107, 108
Blossom end rot of tomato, 142
Blowers, 70
Boron, 75
Brassica juncea L., 50
Brassica oleracea L., 50
Buffer action, 55
Calcium, 75
Capillary action technique, 36
Catalytic elements, 77
Ceramic metal halide, 130
Chelating agent, 78, 79
Chrysanthemum coronarium L., 50
Circulatory methods, 29
Coarse fir sawdust, 66
Coco coir, 65
Compost, 104
Concave panel, 48
Concentric fruit cracking of tomato, 143
Containers, 140
Copper, 76
Cropping patterns, 50
Crushed granite, 66
Cryptotaenia japonica, 32
Cucumis melo L., 50
Cucumis sativus L., 50
Cultural practices, 51
D. R. Hoagland standard solution method, 99
Deep flow technique (DFT), 31
Deep water culture (DWC), 46
Dendrobium nobile, 118
Dendrobium phalaenopsis, 117
Desert hydroponic, 108
Dissolved Oxygen (DO), 87
Downwelling irradiance, 128
Drip (substrate), 92
Drip feeding, 46
Drip system, 44

Dynamic root floating system, 46
Ebb and flow system, 43
Ec meter, 71
Electrical conductivity (EC), 86
Electronic ballasts, 133
Equipments and appliances, 68
Essential plant nutrients, 73, 153
Expanded clay, 61
Fertigation, 95, 97
- advantages, 97
- methods, 96
Fertilizer, 117
Floating technique, 36
Flood cycle, 43
Fluorescent bulbs, 123
Fluorescent light, 123
Flushing, 140
Fog feed technique (FFT), 43
Framework elements, 77
Fresh air, 57
Fruit crooking of cucumber, 144
Fruit crooking, 144
Function of minerals, 76
Grow bag technique, 38
Growing media, 56, 61, 109
Hanging bag technique, 37
High pressure sodium light, 124
High temperature, 140
High-intensity discharge (HID), 132
High-pressure sodium (HPS), 133
Hoaglands solution, 14, 101
Humus, 106
Hydroponic methods for nursery and orchids growing, 109
Hydroponic techniques and their classification, 27
Hydroponics fertilizer mixtures, 93
hydroponics gravel method, 10
Hydroponics
- advantage, 23
- basic requirements, 55
- care and maintenance, 139
- definition, 1
- future prospects of hydroponics, 18
- future strategy, 22
- historical highlights, 14
- history, 6
- limitations, 23, 25
- management requirements, 137
- modern hydroponics, 21
- present status, 16
- semi-hydroponics, 118
- techniques, 28
- why dc people prefer?, 4
Hydroponics
- problems, 141
- remedies, 141
Hydroponics
- suitable orchids, 118
- suitable plants, 151
Hydroton, 61
Ideal temperatures, 112
Incandescent light, 123
Influence on the osmotic pressure of the cells, 77
Insect-pest and disease problem, 141
Ipomoea aquatica Forsk, 50
Iron, 75
Irrigation water quality, 97
Knop, W., 7

Knop's solution, 101
Lactuca sativa L., 50
Lamp placement, 121
Light, 59, 113
- distribution, 131
- spectrums, 119
- working, 126
Lights for plant growth, 122
Liquid hydroponics, 29
Low temperatures, 140
Lycopersicon lycopersicum L., 50
Magnesium, 75
Manganese, 76
Measuring conductivity, 86
Measuring, 89
Media, 117
Metal halide, 133
- light, 123
Micronutrients, 59
Mineral cotton, 62
Mineral nutrients, 58
Moisture content, 139
Moisture, 111
Molarity, 89
Molybdenum, 76
Neutralization, 92
Nitrogen, 74
Non circulating methods, 34
Non standard solutions, 102
Non-recirculating systems, 139
Nursery containers / trays, 111
Nursery period, 114
Nursery raising, 109
Nurtimeter, 71
Nutriculture, 9
Nutrient circulation system, 50
Nutrient film technique (NFT), 29
Nutrient level adjuster and aspirator, 49
Nutrient solution, 52, 56, 73, 77, 79
- constituents, 154
- management, 80, 88
Nutrients
- adjustment, 53
- supply, 114
Nutritional deficiency symptoms in plants, 147
Nutritional disorders, 144
Nutritional toxicity symptoms in plants, 149
Oasis root cubes, 65
Organic and regular fertilizers, 94
Oxygen detection sensor, 68
Passive hydroponics, 116
Perlite, 63
pH, 89
- adjusting, 85
- calculation, 90
- checking, 84
- important?, 82
- level, 81
- meter, 70
Phosphorous, 74
Photon irradiance, 126
Photosynthetically active radiation (PAR), 128
Physiological disorders, 142
Planck's law, 124
plant diseases and their symptoms, 145
Plant light needs, 121
Plant nutrients of hydroponic solution, 74

Planting material production, 113
Planting, 116
POH, 90
Pollinators, 71
Pot technique, 41
Potassium, 75
Primary elements, 73
Protoplasmic elements, 76
PVC pipes, 69
Quantum, 124
Raft cultivation, 46
Rain of photons, 125
Relative humidity, 112
Replacement of nutrient solution, 95
Requirements for nursery raising, 109
Ridged culture bed, 48
Rockwool, 62
Root dipping technique, 34
– for non-root tuber crops, 34
– for root tuber crops, 36
Root mist technique (RMT), 42
Sach's solution, 101
Sand, 66
Scoria, 67
Secondary elements, 73
Seed germination, 113
Semi-hydroponic for growing orchids, 116
Shelter and support, 57
Shrink cracks of bell pepper, 143
Silicate cotton, 62
Slag wool, 62
Solution from the soil, 105
Source of light, 119
Spectroradiometer, 129
Spinacia oleracea L., 50
Sponge nursery technique, 115
Standard nutrient solutions, 99
Stone wool, 62
Structural elements, 73
Sulphur, 74
TDS meter, 71
Temperature, 57
Trace elements, 59
Training and pruning, 135
Transplantation, 117
Trench or trough technique, 40
Upwelling irradiance, 128
Vermiculite, 64
Visible radiations required for photosynthesis, 124
Water pumps, 68
Water quality classes, 155
Water, 58, 117
Wick feeding, 46
Wick system, 45
Zinc, 76